Paul Ramsey, editor

Contemporary Religious Poetry

PAULIST PRESS
New York/Mahwah

APPRECIATIONS

I would like to thank Joseph A. Jackson and his staff (especially R. Neal Coulter and Fay L. Verburg) at the Library of the University of Tennessee at Chattanooga for much assistance; my secretaries Kim Griffin, Nadine Palmer, and Phyllis Worth, for cheerful and careful work; Jeanette Schlaeger for thoughtful suggestions about the Introduction; and Sarah Farmer, Assistant to the President of the DuLeslin Agency, for difficult tasks well done.

Book design by Theresa M. Sparacio.

Library of Congress Cataloging-in-Publication Data

Contemporary religious poetry.

    Includes index.
    1. Religious poetry.   2. Poetry, Modern—20th century.
I. Ramsey, Paul.
PN6110.R4C66   1987   808.81'9382   87-6889
ISBN 0-8091-2883-7 (pbk.)

Published by Paulist Press
997 Macarthur Boulevard
Mahwah, New Jersey 07430

Printed and bound in the United States of America

CONTENTS

iv

EPIGRAMS AND LIGHT VERSE AND KIN
There's a Man Calling: Poems on Words

It Will Take Me Years, Lord: Poems on a Number of Things

A Little Cage of Bone: Poems on Death

ACKNOWLEDGMENTS

The publisher is grateful to The Sterling Lord Agency for permission to reprint "The Invention of Comics," copyright © 1964 by LeRoi Jones (Amiri Baraka); to Coleman Barks for permission to reprint "From 'New Words' "; Daniel Berrigan, S.J. for permission to reprint "The Crucifix"; to Farrar Straus & Giroux Inc. for permission to reprint "Dream Song 64" from 77 *Dream Songs* by John Berryman, copyright © 1959, 1962, 1963, 1964 by John Berryman; to David R. Godine, Boston, for permission to reprint "Two Poems on the Catholic Bavarians" by Edgar Bowers, from *Living Together*, copyright © 1973 by Edgar Bowers; to Kelly Cherry and the Louisiana State University Press for permission to reprint "Love"; to the Ohio University Press for permission to reprint two epigrams from *The Collected Poems and Epigrams of J.V. Cunningham* published by Swallow Press, 1971; to Charles Scribner's Sons for permission to reprint "The Hill" and "The Rescue" by Robert Creeley from *For Love, Poems 1950–1960*, copyright © 1962 by Robert Creeley; to Fazil Hüsnü Dağlarca for permission to reprint "Hollow Echo," "Fire" and "Thought"; to Donald Davie for permission to reprint "Compline" and "Prime"; to Christopher Dornin for permission to reprint "In a Building Named for a Governor"; to Harcourt Brace Jovanovich, Inc. for permission to reprint "Animula" from *Collected Poems 1909–1962* by T.S. Eliot, copyright 1936 by Harcourt Brace Jovanovich, Inc., copyright © 1963, 1964 by T.S. Eliot; to Theodore Enslin for permission to reprint "The Fire Poem"; to Mari Evans for permission to reprint "The Rebel" from *I Am a Black Woman* published by Wm. Morrow, 1970; to Wesleyan University Press for permission to reprint "Exclusive Blue" and "Three Darks Come Together" by Robert Francis, from *The Orb Weaver*, copyright © 1953 by Robert Francis; to The University of Massachusetts Press for permission to reprint "That Dark Other Mountain," "Silent Poem" and "Epitaphs" from *Robert Francis Collected Poems, 1936–1976* (Amherst: University of Massachusetts Press, 1976), copyright © 1944, 1970, 1972, 1974 by Robert Francis; to George Garrett for permission to reprint "Jacob" and "Giant Killer"; to Diane Glancy for permission to reprint "At the Pauwels," "Johnna at the Windmill," "Rahab" and "Wheat"; to New Directions Publishing Corporation for permission to reprint "Tribute to the Angels" by H.D. from *Collected Poems 1912–1944*, copyright © 1982 by the Estate of Hilda Doolittle; to

THIS BOOK IS FOR GEORGE CONNOR
IN FRIENDSHIP AND ESTEEM

"What falls away is always. And is near."

INTRODUCTION

> Three million years
> The Spirit, ranging as it will,
> In sun, in darkness, lives in change.
> Changed and not changed. The spirit hears
> In drifting fern the morning air.
>
> Janet Lewis, "Fossil, 1975"

What is it to be contemporary? What is it to be religious? What is it that poetry does and is? We all know and have some uncertainties about those questions, which fascinate and entice and perplex. When Paulist Press asked me to do an anthology of contemporary religious poetry, I was delighted, realizing soon that fascination and enticement were not enough, since decisions were required.

Compiling an anthology one learns something of the rationality and the arbitrariness of choice. One chooses what he thinks is good and thinks is appropriate to the subject and what works well together—which is reasonable, however able or disabled the actual choosing; yet on some things one just has to decide or set limits. For instance, the anthology consists of poems written or published between 1950 and the present. Why those years? Well, they are a better choice than just this year, and more contemporary to us than, say, 1750-1850; yet there's something arbitrary about any dates set and I've allowed three exceptions to those dates.

To see that is to see what is, in my judgment, a point of some consequence about choice and about language: that there is in both something rational and principled and discussable, and something finally and irreducibly individual and mysterious. We live with both.

Though contemporary in time, the anthology is to some degree and in some ways anti-contemporary in spirit: it largely avoids the kind of poetry I find most typical of the post-modern: self-locked, fragmented, struggled prose, with forced images and lax structures. As the notion of (even) romantic Self collapse pieces writhe selfishly and often unpleasantly, even demanding a desperate and epistemically hopeless uncertainty as the aesthetic ideal. Such a poetic this anthology denies.

I do not intend for the anthology to express my taste, though of course it necessarily and even tautologously does; but have tried to accord my taste to what is genuinely and knowably good. Which is a difficult labor, *worth* trying, in modesty and in hope.

What is it to be religious? That is not really a matter primarily for pleasant or intricate discussion: we are chosen and called and under judgment, and we have our lives to offer.

For purposes for choosing poetry for an anthology, what is it to be religious? The question needs to be answered, again, with some principles, and some plain deciding.

On the one hand, "religious" can be used so generally that a religious anthology becomes just any anthology. For instance, I told one poet about the anthology, and she replied, "Anything which celebrates life is religious, wouldn't you say?" Well, yes, in some senses. What she meant of course was that she didn't write religious poems but would like to have some of her poems included in the anthology: perhaps the ones about love-making replete with imagery from exotic fruits, a kind of *Tom Jones* in miniature. I decided not to oblige.

One could also say that any poetry which implicates value, or implicates relationship(s) between the speaker and reality, is religious poetry, and be right in some senses, even in some important senses. But not in every sense, since we naturally and reasonably call certain poetry religious: Negro spirituals, the poems of George Herbert.

On the other hand, Paulist Press, even though a distinguished Catholic press, wanted a book of contemporary *religious* poetry, not a book of contemporary Catholic poetry or even Christian poetry; I am glad they so chose since otherwise I would have to exclude some relevant poems of our time I like and admire very much.

The poems are Christian, Jewish, and other, including some translations, and with a number of comic poems also. A number of Catholic poets are included—there are a number of very good

2

Catholic poets writing these days—but do not preponderate. The poems included had to have something considered specifically religious or mystical or powerfully ethically relevant, or at least relevant to a given topic, a clear facing of genuine issues. I hope the result is a book which is clearly a collection of religious poetry, but—once again—no simple set of principles will wholly explain all the inclusions or exclusions. Human choice is like that; being religious is like that.

Let me illustrate with two examples. In the section on Death, "A Little Cage of Bone," the poems are all relevant to the topic. "War Memento," by Roger Hecht, is a poem about looking at and brooding on a photograph of a young soldier, dead, somewhere in France, 1915. Here is how the poem ends.

> Something is cockeyed in that death-made grin,
> Suggesting, as it does, nearly a grace
> Or maybe a bravado out of place
> With all the mud soldiers must quarter in.
> But maybe that's the finest way to die
> When what you know is that you have no choice
> Except to carry on and carry on.
> And you smile. You smile beyond all pain.
> Not consciously. But you smile nonetheless.
> Forever. In a snapshot. To no one.

The poem is a memorable facing of death, a severe meditation on death, and thus seemed appropriate even without the hint of grace.

Here is another poem on death, "Each Day," by Sister Maura, in terms of belief more typical of the anthology.

> *Each Day*
> Her face thins almost
> as we watch. Bones
>
> seem larger—grating
> on pillow and sheet

like shells on a hedge
of shore. We speak

more simply in her presence:
a primer of nouns

and verbs. She lets go
of life gently. We

receive from her hands
the victory of belief,

learning the meaning of
our lives from our grief.

Sister Maura writes, in granting permission to republish the poems of hers I chose: "I'm glad that you chose 'Each Day.' When I give a reading, or when readers comment on the book that it is in, it is that poem which they say is the one they remember. It is, I suspect, close to the human heartache that, at some time, we all share."

Which is a lovely reply, and which virtually constitutes a definition of religious poetry: poetry which speaks to our hearts, gives light to our sorrow, and speaks true.

What is it that poetry does and is? It speaks to human motive, what we know about and what we do not know. We know much about why we do things; *and* human motives are often very mysterious. We can say that poetry is in language, sounded, and that poems should *say* what they mean, should be the right and exact locution for what is said, that the sound should echo and be echoed by and be of the meaning. An ideal? Yes, in good poetry approached, sometimes nearly. Poetry is a speaking true, and the truth is of sound and vision and rhetoric meeting to fit the truth a poem conveys and is.

What do we know of human motive? Very much, by common sense, wisdom, science, tradition—and astonishingly little. A psychologist in a prominent position, a good friend of mine, puts it something like this. "People in our society become crazy.

What do we do? We send them to mental hospitals under the care of very learned doctors and psychiatrists and psychologists; we give them many and very sophisticated drugs. What do we achieve? Crazy people who walk funny." Hard? Yes, but much too often true. We would like to do better than that, would we not? We do not, because we don't know how to do better.

Human motive? I shall illustrate by two stories, one my retelling of a fable of Aesop, the second a true tale in a poem of mine.

The fable, by Aesop, is unkind, but then many stories are—literature is often about human meanness, what the theologians call original sin.

Once upon a time there was man who had a child he loved very much. There was a snake, a poisonous snake, who lived not far from his house. One day the man saw the snake in the yard, and since his child played in that yard, he threw sticks to make the snake go away. The snake went away all right, but the snake didn't like having sticks thrown at him. So he planned to get even. He did get even too. He bit the child one day, and the child died. The man buried the child and mourned and mourned. He used to go every day to the child's grave and mourn some more. And he got angrier and angrier at the snake the more he thought about what the snake had done. So he decided to kill the snake. He took an ax and waited and waited outside the hole of the snake's den for the snake to come out. The snake started out and the man swung the ax down hard. But the snake was so fast the man missed the snake and knocked a big chip out of the rock. Then the man went home and worried and worried. He realized the snake might kill him too. So he decided on a truce. He got in touch with the snake and arranged for a parley, so the snake and the man met halfway between their places and sat on two rocks about 10 yards apart, and talked to each other. The man proposed that they forget and forgive and become friends. The snake thought about it, and they talked back and forth for a while. But nothing came of the parley. The snake finally said, "No, it won't work. We can agree on a peace, but every time you see your child's grave you are going to remember and hate me again; and I'll do the same thing every time I look at that big chip out of the rock beside the hole I live in."

Are the gravestone and the chip in the rock symbols? Let's say that they are places, memorable, which tell us something true. Sometimes human motive is intractable; not all problems can be solved.

Here's the other story, as retold in a poem of mine entitled *Fog Days for Great Cranberry Island:*

> And on the south end of the island still mist, then fog.
> There has been mist on the place of the Prussian lady,
> Born Dorethea Albertina
> Called Hannah Caroline.
> When she heard her husband had died in the Arctic,
>   she threw his stuffed seals into the bay.

The story really happened; at least my informants on Great Cranberry Island were quite sure that it really happened, and some of them say that the stuffed seals were rescued by a ship and taken to Boston where some of them are on display in a museum.

I tell that story to students and then ask about motives—fifth grade students, college students, graduate students—and all give some of the same answers: because she loved him, or because she was tired of the seals, or because she resented his being a sea-captain and traveling far and dangerously, or various other notions or variations. Then I ask a trick request, "Well, will someone give the Correct Answer?" and the response normally is resistance, more or sometimes less polite—how can we tell the Correct Answer? or, Who are you to think there is a correct answer? or whatever. But there *is* a correct answer: *we don't know.* Or, as I finish the poem:

> When she heard her husband had died in the Arctic,
>   she threw his stuffed seals in the bay.

> Whether out of grief or hatred, it is too late to say.

We might, with a lucky investigation, be able to say much better whether her motive was grief, or hatred, or both, or boredom or whatever; maybe some letters could be discovered, or whatever. But we know that at best we still would not be wholly sure. Human motive is locked in human breasts, to which chambers with their recesses we have some keys but not every key.

Poetry, then, is an exploration and understanding of human motive. I agree with Yvor Winters that poetry is that and that also the best technique makes a poem which is more true, more appropriate, more richly attuned to the motives discovered and unfolded: I hold, with Winters, that we can know and understand much of human motive and that good poetry expresses such understanding with singularly exacting power; I would also emphasize, perhaps even more than Winters does, how much in human motive remains intractable, mysterious, hard to assess. And that is true of religious poetry as of other poetry: motive and mystery are integral to religious poetry and not every rendition has the same power and integrity and exactitude which the best poetry has.

Poetry is a good, and evil is a privation of good. That theory, from Aquinas and others, does not cover all ground or solve all problems, but is powerful, useful, and in some deep senses true. I am fond of telling students that poetry as such is a good—it is good to invent something, good to express how one feels, good to tell something which will (more or less) interest other people. Some poetry is much better than other poetry, but poetry can only be really bad when it is pretentious, when it claims to be more than it is. Often one needs to tell a student, preferably gently and preferably firmly enough to be listened to, "Your poem is longer than it is." Also, many poems claim to be more than they are. There are pages of illustrations of that in modern poetry journals, pages I shall spare you.

Poems can go wrong by misassessing or misrepresenting human motive. The truth that human motive is often unknowable or mysterious does not mean that anything goes, or that every obscure and bardic gesture about the mystery of things is necessarily valid. In much contemporary poetry, there are many flagrant and smudgy examples of misrepresenting human motive and mystery, or of falsifying claims of what we can say and know, or not say or not know.

A poem, then, can be true about human motive; and there are means of judging how it handles human motive. And how it handles language.

We often say we are fallible; and of course we would agree that in some senses that statement is true. We make mistakes; we are not sure about much which we say; we learn and qualify and change our minds. *But* there's a trick in the language of fallibility, which can make us sound more skeptical or confused or unbelieving than we are. For, if we mean by the statement "We are fallible" that we sometime make mistakes, then by logical parity we should *equally* be entitled to say, "We are infallible," that is, we sometimes get things right, say things which are true. Of course we don't and would be roundly scolded if we did, but the logical point is still relevant, both to our capacity for judging, including judging poetry, and the importance of making relevant distinctions in language in judging and in considering the language in and of poetry.

Poetry should have fit language, language which is a "just and lively image" of what the poem conveys and is, and that fitness, that appropriateness, is long-and-hard-and-good-to-achieve. It is done partially by adjusting language when it does not fit. The process continues, is philosophical, and religious, and human, and poetic, and gets somewhere.

Newspapers often tell us that someone died unexpectedly. A good friend of mine once commented upon reading such a story "No one ever dies unexpectedly." We know what the newspaper meant; but our sense of language and our lives and deaths are clearer after hearing the comment. We do expect to die, and should learn to die well. Religious discourse, including poetry, has told us so for a long time.

Language does and does not fit reality, and the process of accommodation is perpetual, possible, fruitful, and our task. John Dryden tells us that poetry should be a just and lively *image* of reality, and Alexander Pope tells us that sound should be an echo to the sense. Note that the only way it can be that is for the sense to be in some way a sound. Echoes are sounds reflecting sounds. Language and meaning and reality stand apart and mutually enter.

Richard M. Gale, a philosopher responding to Henri Bergson's charge that our symbols distort reality, writes (*The Philosophy of Time*, ed. Richard M. Gale, Atlantic Highlands, NJ: Humanities Press, 1968, p. 392) that Bergson's claim is true only in the trivial sense that "symbols are qualitatively different from their referents: the word 'amorous,' for example, is not itself warm and passionate. One does not say a physicist's vector diagram is a vicious distortion of reality because it does not get up and run around the room." But if a poet writes an amorous poem, we want it to be warm and passionate (or otherwise appropriate); and if a poet should do a vector diagram it *should* gallop about the room. We do what we can, as best (at our best) as we may.

Religious discourse or poetry is apt to provoke special claims and disclaimers, virtual frenzies of timidity. The Bible is not mealy-mouthed; theories of religious language often are. We are often told that our language for talking about God is inadequate and that in speaking about God we need metaphors, no metaphor wholly sufficing. Metaphor is odd stuff and hard to talk about, and one can overrate or underrate the place that 'metaphor' (meaning this or that or whatever) has in our discourse. For instance, the term "literal" is a metaphor. But we still can speak. When a Christian says, "Jesus of Nazareth *is* God," the statement is in no sense metaphorically intended. We mean that it is true. And, certainly, it does not follow from our nervousness about metaphor and language and such that anything equally goes in speaking about God.

Language is language. The word "rabbit" does not exhaust rabbitness or *visibly* include each rabbit, born or yet to be born, but that does not mean that we are free to substitute words at random for the word "rabbit." I suggest that we treat God as well linguistically as we treat rabbits.

Karl Barth says in *The Faith of the Church* (ed. Jean-Louis Leuba, trans. Gabriel Vahanian, New York: Meridian Books, 1958, p. 47) that God's hands are literal, ours metaphorical (how dare we call these paws *hands?*), an astonishingly wise thing to say. We are the "metaphor," God the reality. We are the vapor, God the Rock.

Aristotle writes in the *Poetics* (trans. Leon Golden, commentary by O. B. Hardison, Englewood Cliffs, N.J.: Prentice-Hall, 1968, p. 38) "to scatter seed is to sow, but the scattering of the sun's rays has no name. But the act of sowing in regard to grain bears an analogous relation to the sun's dispersing of its rays, and so we have the phrase 'sowing the god-created fire.' " Aristotle perceives a hole in language and promptly closes it. The sun of which he speaks sows light, on the problem of understanding our language and our knowledge and our faith, even now.

Some philosophy recent and older gives me hope, the work of Wittgenstein and Peter Geach and Max Black and Paul Holmer and G. E. M. Anscombe and Aristotle and Aquinas and John Wisdom and others, who have helped us to see how language can be used to clarify, to strengthen, to understand, not just to speculate and entangle and doubt. The linguistic movement in philosophy early on was deeply positivistic and anti-Christian; it has changed and grown since.

I am hopeful philosophically, a Christian in Faith, and I think the two meet, and rejoice. One of our tasks is to make our language more adequate by thought, distinction, reflection, caring, love.

Poems praise or blame: panegyric and satire are the most fundamental kinds of poetry, and of religious poetry that is also manifestly true: celebration and lamentation are major modes, and abudantly exemplified in the tradition. We think, with some reason, that modern poetry is more apt to lament (or to whine) than to praise; it is good to know that the tradition of praise still lives. Thus, in an example from the anthology, Ann Stanford writes of and partly quotes Anne Hutchinson:

> O the depth of God's grace
> The height of his salvation
> The overflowing of his goodness
> The mystery of his Covenant.

He who hung the stars as lamps
Cast out chaos, lit the sun,
And flung forth meadows and fields.
Does he not care for us?

He gave us the Son
And the Spirit to dwell in us
Christ freely gives saving faith
And the Spirit speaks to us.

I think the Soule be nothing but Light.

Anne Hutchinson got into trouble for making statements such as the last, but the sentence is splendid poetry.

The voice of lamentation is also heard in the land, as in David Rosenberg's potent modern translations and redactions from the Hebrew of the Book of Lamentations.

I was fenced in like sheep
I was locked in an empty room

I was bound in chains
I could not turn around

I could not stand up to pray
he had turned away

Light speaks, and sorrow is heard.

The title "By Light and Sorrow" of a section of this book comes from a poem by Karol Wojtyla, better known to us as Pope John Paul II. It is a fine poem (in translation: it sounds beautiful in Polish, a language of which I fear I am innocent); it sums some themes I have spoken of.

Song of the Brightness of Water

Even this depth—I came only to draw water
in a jug—so long ago, this brightness

still clings to my eyes—the perception I found,
and so much empty space, my own,
reflected in the well.

Yet it is good. I can never take all of you
into me. Stay then as mirror in the well.
Leaves and flowers remain, and each astonished gaze
brings them down
to my eyes transfixed more by light
than by sorrow.

    I ended my search for poems for the anthology more in touch with light than with sorrow, though both are necessarily and recurrently present. I got gloomy, I still get gloomy some, not to mention enraged— at much in the modern literary scene, which I shall leave charitably undefined for now (I have spoken of some of the problems often in my writing and reviews). Finishing the anthology I was cheered: there is, in my judgment, to my taste if you will—certainly to my sober pleasure and my relaxed delight—much good religious poetry being written: sober, comic, exploring, skillful, lucid, various.

    This introduction speaks of religion and motive and language, what they are, how they work and refract within contemporary religious poetry, and gives some examples. The Pope's beautiful poem sums some things I have said and would say: the search and discovery and rejoicing and sorrow which is and is in and of our religion; the motive to serve Our Lord, to explore and allow-to-be-mended our bruised hearts; in language which reaches and fails to reach in its very resounding, and yet can be known. The perception discovers our empty space, our unknowing, yet is not lost therein; and what we see of God refreshes our natural vision of leaf and flower, in sorrow and in abundant light. Good poetry can help that seeing.

Against the Wind of Time

Archibald MacLeish

SIGNATURE FOR TEMPO

I

THINK that this world against the wind of
   time
Perpetually falls the way a hawk
Falls at the wind's edge but is motionless—

Think that this silver snail the moon will climb
All night upon time's curving stalk
That as she climbs bends, bends beneath her—
                              Yes
And think that we remember the past time.

II

These live people,
These more
Than three dimensional
By time protracted edgewise into heretofore
People,
How shall we bury all
These queer-shaped people,
In graves that have no more
Than three dimensions?
Can we dig
With such sidlings and declensions

As to coffin bodies big
With memory?
And how
Can the earth's contracted Now
Enclose these knuckles and this crooked knee
Sprawled over hours of a sun long set?

Or do these bones forget?

III

Borne
Landward on relinquishing seas,
Worn
By the sliding of water

Whom time goes over wave by wave, do I lie
Drowned in a crumble of surf at the sea's
    edge?—

And wonder now what ancient bones are these
That flake on sifting flake
Out of deep time have shelved this shallow ledge
    Where the waves break—

Allen Tate

SONNETS AT CHRISTMAS
1934

I

This is the day His hour of life draws near,
Let me get ready from head to foot for it
Most handily with eyes to pick the year
For small feed to reward a feathered wit.
Some men would see it an epiphany
At ease, at food and drink, others at chase
Yet I, stung lassitude, with ecstasy
Unspent argue the season's difficult case
So: Man, dull critter of enormous head,
What would he look at in the coiling sky?
But I must kneel again unto the Dead
While Christmas bells of paper white and red,
Figured with boys and girls spilt from a sled,
Ring out the silence I am nourished by.

II

Ah, Christ, I love you rings to the wild sky
And I must think a little of the past:
When I was ten I told a stinking lie
That got a black boy whipped; but now at last
The going years, caught in an accurate glow,
Reverse like balls englished upon green baize—

Let them return, let the round trumpets blow
The ancient crackle of the Christ's deep gaze.
Deafened and blind, with senses yet unfound,
Am I, untutored to the after-wit
Of knowledge, knowing a nightmare has no sound;
Therefore with idle hands and head I sit
In late December before the fire's daze
Punished by crimes of which I would be quit.

T. S. Eliot

ANIMULA

'Issues from the hand of God, the simple soul'
To a flat world of changing lights and noise,
To light, dark, dry or damp, chilly or warm;
Moving between the legs of tables and of chairs,
Rising or falling, grasping at kisses and toys,
Advancing boldly, sudden to take alarm,
Retreating to the corner of arm and knee,
Eager to be reassured, taking pleasure
In the fragrant brilliance of the Christmas tree,
Pleasure in the wind, the sunlight and the sea;
Studies the sunlit pattern on the floor
And running stags around a silver tray;
Confounds the actual and the fanciful
Content with playing-cards and kings and queens,
What the fairies do and what the servants say.
The heavy burden of the growing soul
Perplexes and offends more, day by day;
Week by week, offends and perplexes more
With the imperatives of 'is and seems'
And may and may not, desire and control.
The pain of living and the drug of dreams
Curl up the small soul in the window seat
Behind the *Encyclopaedia Britannica*.
Issues from the hand of time the simple soul
Irresolute and selfish, misshapen, lame,
Unable to fare forward or retreat,
Fearing the warm reality, the offered good,
Denying the importunity of the blood,

Leaving disordered papers in a dusty room;
Living first in the silence after the viaticum.

Pray for Gutierrez, avid of speed and power,
For Boudin, blown to pieces,
For this one who made a great fortune,
And that one who went his own way.
Pray for Floret, by the boarhound slain between the yew trees,
Pray for us now and at the hour of our birth.

By Light and Sorrow

Daniel Berrigan

THE CRUCIFIX
(for an eighty-sixth birthday)

I

I remember today a Quebec roadside, the crucifix
raised crude as life among farming people,
its shadow creeping, dawn and twilight, over their lives.
Among wains, haycocks and men it moved like a savior.

So old, so scored by their winters, it had been staked out
perhaps by a band of ruffians on first Good Friday.
The way it endured, time would have bruised his fist in striking
   it.

What time had done, breaking the bones at knee and wrist,
washing the features blank as quarry stone,
turning the legs to spindles, stealing the eyes

was only to plant forever its one great gesture
deeper in furrow, heave it high above rooftops.

Where time had done his clumsy worst, cracking its heart,
hollowing its breast inexorably,—he opened this Burning-glass
to hold the huge landscape: crops, houses and men, in Its fire.

II

He was irremovably there, nailing down the landscape,
more permanent than any mountain time could bring down

or frost alter face of. He could not be turned aside
from his profound millennial prayer: not by birds
moved wonderfully to song on that cruel bough:
not by sun, standing compassionately at right hand or left.

Let weathers tighten or loosen his nails: he was vowed to stand.
Northstar took rise from his eyes, learned constancy of him.

Let cloudburst break like judgment, sending workmen
     homeward
whipping their teams from field, down the rutted road to barn

still his body took punishment like a mainsail
bearing the heaving world onward to the Father.

And men knew nightlong: in the clear lovely morning he will
     be there,
not to be pulled down from landscape, never from his people's
     hearts.

Edgar Bowers

TWO POEMS ON THE CATHOLIC BAVARIANS

1

The fierce and brooding holocaust of faith
This people conquered, which no edict could,
And wove its spirit stiff and rich like cloth
That many years ago was soaked in blood.

Their minds are active only in their hands
To check and take the labor of the hills,
To furnish nature its precise demands
And bear its harshness as it seems God wills.

But holy passion hurts them in each season
To blend themselves with nature if they can;
They find in well known change enough of reason
To worship Him in it as Him in Man.

Thus in the summer on the Alpine heights
A deity of senseless wrath and scorn
Is feasted through the equinoctial nights
As though a savage Christ were then reborn.

Up from the floors of churches in December
The passion rises to a turbulence
Of darkness such as threatens to dismember
The mind submerged in bestial innocence.

And Druid shades with old dementia fraught
Possess the souls they had accounted loss
And join their voices, raging and distraught,
About the curious symbol of the cross.

2

I know a wasted place high in the Alps
Called Witches' Kitchen. There the sun all day
With aberrant change of shadows plagues the eyes,
And when the equinoctial moon has play

Upon the beast-like monoliths of stone,
The blood runs cold as its old passions rise
To haunt the memory of what we are
And what we do in worshipping brute skies.

Below this waste of spirit and of mind
The village Holy Blood with ordered care
Was founded on deep meadows. Yearly, sheep
Are brought to graze in summer pastures there.

Its people sow and harvest grain together
Between the comings of the winter's ice,
And when they stop to take a quick sprung flower,
Its being and their gesture will suffice

To balance what they are and what are not.
And if we turn to look within the town
Upon a wall we find the stencilled group
Of Mary, John, and others taking down

The body of their Master from the tree.
And just at dusk the daylight's weakened pace
Shades the blue chalk of Mary's robe with red;
And her faint tears are red upon His face.

Kelly Cherry

LOVE

In the attention it pays to each detail,
In its frailty and flexibility,
In the way it seeks out a new trail
While stumbling repeatedly upon the old,

You will know love, and know
That what it cannot fail to do
Is render even this late scene
In all its abundance.

The red-tailed hawk overhead,
Spongy moss springing from wet bark,
The sound of your own walking
Through these autumnal woods.

Robert Creeley

THE HILL

It is sometime since I have been
to what it was had once turned me backwards,
and made my head into
a cruel instrument.

It is simple
to confess. Then done,
to walk away, walk away,
to come again.

But that form, I must answer,
is dead in me, completely.
and I will not allow it
to reappear—

Saith perversity, the willful,
the magnanimous cruelty,
which is in me
like a hill.

THE RESCUE

The man sits in a timelessness
with the horse under him in time
to a movement of legs and hooves
upon a timeless sand.

Distance comes in from the foreground
present in the picture as time
he reads outward from
and comes from that beginning.

A wind blows in
and out and all about the man
as the horse ran
and runs to come in time.

A house is burning in the sand.
A man and horse are burning.
The wind is burning.
They are running to arrive.

H. D.

from *TRIBUTE TO THE ANGELS*

[Mary]

We have seen her
the world over,

Our Lady of the Goldfinch,
Our Lady of the Candelabra,

Our Lady of the Pomegranate,
Our Lady of the Chair;

we have seen her, an empress,
magnificent in pomp and grace,

and we have seen her
with a single flower

or a cluster of garden-pinks
in a glass beside her;

we have seen her snood
drawn over her hair,

or her face set in profile
with the blue hood and stars;

we have seen her head bowed down
with the weight of a domed crown,

or we have seen her, a wisp of a girl
trapped in a golden halo;

we have seen her with arrow, with doves
and a heart like a valentine;

we have seen her in fine silks imported
from all over the Levant,

and hung with pearls brought
from the city of Constantine;

we have seen her sleeve
of every imaginable shade

of damask and figured brocade;
it is true,

the painters did very well by her;
it is true, they missed never a line

of the suave turn of the head
or subtle shade of lowered eye-lid

or eye-lids half-raised; you find
her everywhere (or did find),

in cathedral, museum, cloister,
at the turn of the palace stair.

We see her hand in her lap,
smoothing the apple-green

or the apple-russet silk;
we see her hand at her throat,

fingering a talisman
brought by a crusader from Jerusalem;

we see her hand unknot a Syrian veil
or lay down a Venetian shawl

on a polished table that reflects
half a miniature broken column;

we see her stare past a mirror
through an open window,

where boat follows slow boat on the lagoon;
there are white flowers on the water.

But none of these, none of these
suggest her as I saw her,

though we approach possibly
something of her cool beneficence

in the gracious friendliness
of the marble sea-maids in Venice,

who climb the altar-stair
at *Santa Maria dei Miracoli*,

or we acclaim her in the name
of another in Vienna,

Maria von dem Schnee,
our Lady of the Snow.

Donald Davie

from *HORAE CANONICAE*

COMPLINE

Now I lay me down to sleep
Perhaps not to wake, and I am alone in the house!
How much alone in whatever house of bone,
Suddenly I love my fellow creatures
So much, though for that the hour was Sext, was noon.
I tell you over feverishly, my loved ones,
You are my own, you are? My own! My own?

IN A BUILDING NAMED FOR A GOVERNOR

I changed a grown man's clothes on a stripped ward.
"I'm Daddy," he echoed someone not there.
His throne was a bench. His children were rags.
His skills had wasted a new year. His lord
Was the room itself. His friends understood
Only simple dangers and plain commands.
One lived in a corner and scared the rest.
He was blind. One broke fingers with his wheels.
One had broken his own legs seven times
To make people obey him, and they did.
One said, "Pray for you. Pray for you," all day.
I hoped he would. Few others ever pray
For few others. But he'll say, "Pray for you,"
When judgment comes by horse up the stone ramp,
And men change and feed themselves or they die.
Some will succeed. The clean man struggled to bed.
"For you, for you, for you, for you," he said.

Theodore Enslin

THE FIRE POEM

1

Note that the fire
    consumes not itself,
but what is cast there:
                Into it.

   or
Note: That the fire
               consumes
only what is brought to it.
                  Note
from Eckhart, who had watched fires,
warmed body and spirit there
—spiritu in corpore—
                  who had seen
clearly that the natural life
               relates
to the divine
        or given
      through
not always a correlation.
It is dangerous to assume
            the ecology
of these things.
            But it is the time of fire
and its sometime fuel.

That at night
the fire
      sinks
         down
is rescued
       only
by the morning log
in nick of time
           to
renew itself
        go out
through radiance
the high intention
glowing/
       /in fruition.

At Twelfth Night's burning
of the greens
        there is
more than cleanliness:
           To destroy
more than the ritual implies—
some old urge
        ancestry
to show the face of one man
to another
        in the darkness.
That fire purifies
          is no mistake:
fructifies
nor that it claims the sun
light

        in a little place—
this hard-cored-coal.

                        4

But to break loose again—
the finger length
                flame
following
            underground
the source of roots—
suddenly
        whirls up
catches in the high trees
a crown fire
           rising
with the wind.

                        5

        or one
            small
        votive
            light

Robert Francis

SILENT POEM

backroad   leafmold   stonewall   chipmunk
underbrush   grapevine   woodchuck   shadblow

woodsmoke   cowbarn   honeysuckle   woodpile
sawhorse   bucksaw   outhouse   wellsweep

backdoor   flagstone   bulkhead   buttermilk
candlestick   ragrug   firedog   brownbread

hilltop   outcrop   cowbell   buttercup
whetstone   thunderstorm   pitchfork   steeplebush

gristmill   millstone   cornmeal   waterwheel
watercress   buckwheat   firefly   jewelweed

gravestone   groundpine   windbreak   bedrock
weathercock   snowfall   starlight   cockcrow

THAT DARK OTHER MOUNTAIN

My father could go down a mountain faster than I
Though I was first one up.
Legs braced or with quick steps he slid the gravel slopes
Where I picked cautious footholds.

Black, Iron, Eagle, Doublehead, Chocorua,
Wildcat and Carter Dome—

He beat me down them all. And that last other
   mountain.
And that dark other mountain.

THREE DARKS COME DOWN TOGETHER

Three darks come down together,
Three darks close in around me:
Day dark, year dark, dark weather.

They whisper and conspire,
They search me and they sound me
Hugging my private fire.

Day done, year done, storm blowing,
Three darknesses impound me
With dark of white snow snowing.

Three darks gang up to end me,
To browbeat and dumbfound me.
Three future lights defend me.

George Garrett

GIANT KILLER

I've heard the case for clarity. I know
much can be said for fountains and for certain bells
that seem to wring the richness from the day
like juice of sweetest fruits, say, plums and tangerines,
grapes and pineapples and peaches. There are so many
ripe things, crushed, will sing on the thrilled tongue.

I know the architecture of the snow's composed
of multitudes of mirrors whose strict forms
prove nothing if they do not teach that God loves all
things classic, balanced and austere in grace
as, say, Tallchief in *Swan Lake*, a white thing floating
like the feather of a careless angel, dropped.

But there are certain of God's homely creatures that
I can love no less—the shiny toad, a fine hog fat in mud,
sporting like Romans at the baths, a mockingbird
whose true song is like oboes out of tune, the crow
who, cawing above a frozen winter field,
had just the note of satire and contempt.

I will agree that purity's a vital matter,
fit for philosophers and poets to doze upon. I'll agree
the blade is nobler than a rock. But then I think
of David with Goliath, how he knelt
and in a cloudy brook he felt for stones.
I like that disproportion. They were well thrown.

JACOB

Years and scars later
I finally learn
all angels travel
under assumed names.

Diane Glancy

AT THE PAUWELS

I walked on the edge of the churchyard, my shoes hurt my
    feet. I'd come from a farmhouse down the road
      into the cemetery, marked the lot.

Their child died in an overturned tractor and treebark like
    the parched, cracked earth, was death, the coming of
      death, and its overtaking. The bruised heel

In the shadow of the tree. Their farmhouse painted blue
    and yellow, strange people, not often in church.
      He sat with his arms folded on the table, his head
        on his arms.

I still lived in grandma's farmhouse that Mr. Gollihar, the
    Rifes, and Reverend Herpel had restored. The barn,
      sheds, and fields belonged to others.

Hetter had put her hand on me, and prayed that the ministry
    would pass unto me. The drystalks rattle at our
      passing, Frehauf once said.

I put my hand on Pauwels and prayed, waited on the Lord,
    like dinner at Herman's. Pauwels had heard the gospel,
      now he knew the father's glory in the
        son.

JOHNNA AT THE WINDMILL

Hollis laughed
that my great-great-great-grandfather must
have crossed the Atlantic in the crow's nest.
Why else would I have climbed the windmill
all those times, but for that
ancestral trait carried over?

And from the
windmill, I watched the farthest point
with my great-great-great-grandfather;
he had looked for land from the mast, but I
searched
for water.

RAHAB

Gollihar
Burned the winter grass from his fields.

At dusk,
the fires made a jagged flame across the dim edge of
horizon—

like Rahab's scarlet thread on the wall of Jericho.

WHEAT

The combines crossed the wheat field,
their slatted wheels turned back the flaxen stalks—

turned back the field-trees
and grain elevator,

turned back the prairie wind
with thunder in it.

There was always more going on, David,
than we knew.

O. B. Hardison, Jr.

MARINA

I think of the sea changing and changing.
There is a long swell moving in from the Azores
Awash on the gray sand.
The sky unfolds into the water.
At Holden, Long Beach, Wilmington, Ocean Isle, Hatteras,
  Nags Head
The Outer Banks are ringing with explosions of light.
Clouds blossom in the water and the shore flames with the glory
  of their opening
As though God were making the world again.
Here I am, where the gentle sea touches the land,
And every name is new,
And every name is another name for the sea.

STELLA MARIS

Star of the sea, surest point of brightness,
In the long darkness, compass point
For the poor traveler to whom, wild with longing,
Despairing of home, the skies for a moment open
(Mother of God, he says, let them not close)
To disclose that point, that quiet point
On which the nine spheres turn and their intelligence,
And sing, and rightly, only for you.
Stella Maris. Always bright. Always, never changing, yourself.

Roger Hecht

WAR MEMENTO
(SOMEWHERE IN FRANCE 1915)

A boy with yellow hair, his clothes in place,
Lies stretched on mud, his strange face to the sun.
Behind him, one stripped tree, a small shell hole
More than a yard wide, one wall of a house.
And looking at the boy, a standing man
With perfect blankness set on both his eyes.
The rifle in his hands looks fresh with oil.
He stands. He stares. Nothing, nothing at all
Changes or moves. Such is the photograph
Of something ordinary in a war.
What here is awry? Plain humanity
Should have blanketed the corpse. Now the laugh
That slits his face seems a disturbing glare
Or filthy joke the dead boy settled for
The moment when he had to take the death
That mocks by laughter all eternity.
I stare, unable to salute farewell
Or give this dying any epitaph.

Something is cockeyed in that death-made grin,
Suggesting, as it does, nearly a grace
Or, maybe, a bravado out of place
With all the mud soldiers must quarter in.
But maybe that's the finest way to die
When what you know is that you have no choice

Except to carry on and carry on.
And so you smile, you smile beyond all pain.
Not consciously. But you smile nonetheless.
Forever. In a snapshot. To no one.

M. L. Hester

THE LIGHTNING ROD SALESMAN

Say what you want about doctors or priests.
I saved lives in fifteen states
with a smile and a sample case.

It wasn't fear that sold the rods,
but my calm handshake, dispelling thunder.
It said: these metal tubes
can circumvent God's righteous wrath.

But I wonder—all that lightning
with no proper place to strike,
running itself with a grudge
into the harmless ground—
where does it really go?

Sometimes on stormy nights I wait,
safe in my living room,
my samples standing silent guard
on the roof, the chimney's top . . .

Everything is grounded, true. But
I still brace myself for the flash,
for the rising hum
to pull me up by my shirt and shake me
like a new-discovered enemy, or perhaps
a brother thought and wished long dead.

LeRoi Jones [Inamu Amiri Baraka]

THE INVENTION OF COMICS

I am a soul in the world: in
the world of my soul the whirled
light from the day
the sacked land
of my father.

In the world, the sad
nature of
myself. In myself
nature is sad. Small
prints of the day. Its
small dull fires. Its
sun, like a greyness
smeared on the dark.

The day of my soul, is
the nature of that
place. It is a landscape. Seen
from the top of a hill. A
grey expanse; dull fires
throbbing on its seas.

The man's soul, the complexion
of his life. The menace
of its greyness. The
fire, throbs, the sea
moves. Birds shoot
from the dark. The edge

of the waters lit
darkly for the moon.

And the moon, from the soul. Is
the world, of the man. The man
and his sea, and its moon, and
the soft fire throbbing. Kind
death. O
my dark and sultry
love.

Donald Justice

AN ELEGY IS PREPARING ITSELF

There are pines that are tall enough
Already. In the distance,
The whining of saws; and needles,
Silently slipping through the chosen cloth.
The stone, then as now, unfelt,
Perfectly weightless. And certain words,
That will come together to mourn,
Waiting, in their dark clothes, apart.

THE SNOWFALL

The classic landscapes of dreams are not
More pathless, though footprints leading nowhere
Would seem to prove that a people once
Survived for a little even here.

Fragments of a pathetic culture
Remain, the lost mittens of children,
And a single, bright, detasseled snow cap,
Evidence of some frantic migration.

The landmarks are gone. Nevertheless,
There is something familiar about this country.
Slowly now we begin to recall

The terrible whispers of our elders
Falling softly about our ears
In childhood, never believed till now.

SONNET: THE WALL
For John Berryman

The walls surrounding them they never saw;
The angels, often. Angels were as common
As birds or butterflies, but looked more human.
As long as the wings were furled, they felt no awe.
Beasts, too, were friendly. They could find no flaw
In all of Eden: this was the first omen.
The second was the dream which woke the woman.
She dreamed she saw the lion sharpen his claw.
As for the fruit, it had no taste at all.
They had been warned of what was bound to happen.
They had been told of something called the world.
They had been told and told about the wall.
They saw it now; the gate was standing open.
As they advanced, the giant wings unfurled.

Peter Levi

from *PANCAKES FOR THE QUEEN OF BABYLON*

VIII

A city built in darkness and cold air

    cold fire

the cold rattle of sparrows and milk-bottles
and early feet already in the street

Towering tomorrows
wade ankle-deep in a groundmist of gardens.

in any man in his life in the meditation of his heart

    your body, my body

There are five pure colours
and one impure religion.

Darkness.
Far away the mountains are snow-speckled.
The shadow edges forward,
it marks the giant doors of the bus station.

    Dressed in blue canvas the nightwind disperses a
        smell of
rain of diesels and of sleep. This flurry is colder than
    the last.

wrapped in a heavy coat my younger brother
vanishes quickly in the smoking fog.

This city is a matter of darkness.

uncertain if my brother ever sleeps
what my life is or does what my life is

Fumes of a dying nest of newspapers,
upstairs alone in an abandoned house.

at other times
when the horsechestnuts lighted their candles

clamour of metal in the snow and mist.

their bodies are like water their life summer,
the sunlight will be rumpling everything

We have come back.

Handfuls of leaves are painting a whole street.

                              and in the nettles where
alleys of shadows and humidity
step downward into ranker water-scenes

The stone itself is
the stones are beginning.

The trees have broken into their new youth.
Houses overhanging rivers
                              suddenly
break out into

Ragged red banners are appearing.

Your body and my body.

Last week, at the railway station,
you said. Do you remember.
There was a kind of smoky smell of sun.
For us, to whom nothing has been promised.

I can believe in nothing but in God.

my life is in this belief

my life is in this city

Janet Lewis

THE APRIL HILL

"She did not climb the April hill."
Aye, did she so,
But in no way
In which we're wont to say
Climbed she that hill.

She climbed a farther hill
More fair than show
The meadows here
Into an air more clear,
A light more still.

She climbed the April hill.
We saw her go
Clear in our view
Up to the edge of blue,
And upward still.

COUNTRY BURIAL

After the words of the magnificence and doom,
After the vision of the splendor and the fear,
They go out slowly into the flowery meadow,
Carrying the casket, and lay it on the earth
By the grave's edge. The daisies bend and straighten
Under the trailing skirts, and serious faces
Look with faint relief, and briefly smile.

Into this earth the flesh and wood shall melt
And under these familiar common flowers
Flow through the earth they both have understood
By sight and touch and daily sustenance.
And this is comforting;
For heaven is a blinding radiance where
Leaves are no longer green, nor water wet,
Milk white, soot black, nor winter weather cold,
And the eyeless vision of the Almighty Face
Brings numbness to the untranslatable heart.

FOSSIL, 1975

Changed and not changed. Three million years.
This sunlight-summoned little fern
Closed in a cenotaph of silt
Lies in my hand, secret and safe.
In quiet dark transformed to stone,
Cell after cell to crystal grown,
The pattern stays, the substance gone.
Changed and not changed. Three million years
The Spirit, ranging as it will,
In sun, in darkness, lives in change.
Changed and not changed. The spirit hears
In drifting fern the morning air.

A LULLABY

Lullee, lullay,
I could not love thee more
If thou wast Christ the King.
Now tell me, how did Mary know
That in her womb should sleep and grow
The Lord of everything?

Lullee, lullay,
An angel stood with her
Who said, "That which doth stir
Like summer in thy side
Shall save the world from sin.
Then stable, hall and inn
Shall cherish Christmas-tide."

Lullee, lullay,
And so it was that Day.
And did she love Him more
Because an angel came
To prophesy His name?
Ah no, not so,
She could not love Him more,
But loved Him just the same.
Lullee, lullee, lullay.

John Logan

FOR MY DAUGHTER

This red
          Italian hand
blown glass
                    vase
narrow as the very young
stem
          of your age,
Theresa, has a flame
shaped
               flaw
white
          as the stark
movement in
                         my scarlet brain
when
          I think forever
(like a curse deliver-
                              ed *to* me)
of the fire screaming in the christmas tree
New Year's Day night
you fled tall
               with your beautiful
fire
          colored hair
(your face white
even in the heat)
into the flaw-
                    ed snow

with its wrong
        red tongues.

from A SHORT LIFE OF THE HERMIT

He told the crowd "The devils
Crash and rumble as boys
Or thieves, are tall as roofs
And heavy. Their mouths are black
The eyes are dead as the agate
Dawn. Their stony paws
Click on the eggs of souls.
But at the whispered name they shriek,
Vanishing with a cast of heat."

                    *   *   *

Once he made a basket
Out of stems of reed
And felt a gentle tugging
In his hand; and met
A giant with the withered
Face of birds and long
And whitened arms of men,
Which at the secret name snapped
Into sticks of reed.

And once he felt his ghost
Stand aside, saw it
Climb the lower hills of air
To meet the fallen Lord
Whose morning beauty still
Shivers in the brightness there.

from A CYCLE FOR MOTHER CABRINI

2. iv.

Saint, who overlaps
Our lives who knows the mishaps
Of our times the flaws
Of men no longer outlaws

Even; who knows our schools
Our stores our gods and business rules
Saw charts rise and fall
In your chromium hospital—

You helped shape our city
And the city in the sky:
Help me shape your beauty
In this scarred and remade sky.

from THE DEATH OF SOUTHWELL

Topcliffe's horses shake
The steam of gray morning; men
Grow sad with cold.
The house is sketched well-marked
Where mass is said. What argument:
The traitor's vested. Take him.
Cloak his colors! These horses
Scream. Now load his books,
His papist images; and this
Damned altar furniture
That burnishes with sun!

HANGMAN SITS IN TYBURN TREE
PREACHER SAYS HIS HOMILY
NOW HIS CART IS PULLED EMPTY
HANGMAN HANGED HIM AWKWARDLY
LOOK THE PREACHER'S HAND IS FREE
BLESSES HANGMAN BLESSES ME
HERE'S A FRIEND TO PULL THE KNEE
GHOST NOW LEAVES THE YOUNG BODY
THIS POET SAINT WAS THIRTY THREE
THE HANGMAN MOANS IN TYBURN TREE

John Macoubrie

BOETHIUS AT CAVALZERO

If, as Plato called them, shadows,
Only shadows, always fading,
Are the objects of our knowledge
(Or what we suppose for knowledge)
Vainly searched in this degraded
World of semblance, world of exile,
World where wanton Fortune governs—
Why, then, we must search beyond them,
Search beyond these fading shadows!

In this dungeon where I languish,
Bound unjustly, light denied me,
I have brooded much upon them,
Much upon the rule of Fortune
(Other despots all her puppets),
And now turn again with Plato
Toward that world of light and knowledge,
Our forgotten homeland, whither
Dame Philosophy has led me.

If our homeland then be elsewhere,
Shining in the light of Godhead,
In the light eternal shining,
Where the just obtain full knowledge
(Unobscured by any shadow)
Who behold the very fountain,
Why should I complain of dungeon
Solitude or dungeon darkness?
There my solace, come whatever.

Sister M. Madeleva, C.S.C.

CANDLEMAS DAY

Through what obscure, half-comprehending night
Thou shinest, Christ, for light!
Candle and flame Thou art,
Set in the candelabrum of my heart.

FROM AN AFTERNOON CALLER

I called at your
New house today
To hear the words
You do not say;

To watch the eyes
I cannot see,
The hands you do not
Give to me.

I waited there
A quiet while
In the lost wonder
Of your smile,

And found a home
Austere and new
That has enshrined
And hallowed you.

I love this house
Where you are dead.
Your new grave leaves me
Comforted.

Roland Mathias

GOD IS

God is who questions me
Of my tranquillity
And works against the grain
To raise up Cain.

What is this mark I set
On each sleek head? The hot
Manifest of dislike or ice-
Pick of justice?

What are these books, this room
In which I sit so long?
Are we not met to cry
'Lord, justify!'

DEPARTURE IN MIDDLE AGE

The hedges are dazed as cock-crow, heaps of leaves
Brushed back to them like a child's hair
After a sweat, and clouds as recently bundled
Out of the hollows whimper a little in the conifers higher up.
I am the one without tears, cold
And strange to myself as a stepfather encountered
For the first time in the passage from the front door.

But I cannot go back, plump up the pillow and shape
My sickness like courage. I have spent the night in a shiver:

Usk water passing now was a chatter under the Fan
When the first cold came on. They are all dead, all,
Or scattered, father, mother, my pinafore friends,
And the playground's echoes have not waited for my return.
Exile is the parcel I carry, and you know this,
Clouds, when you drop your pretences and the hills clear.

Sister Maura, S.S.N.D.

THE CREATION OF LIGHT

God sits on the firmament arch
above the world. Beneath his awful
and benignant word the Spirit
winged as a thin bush
and veiled from its own brightness
moves over deep water-like waves
the monk has margined into blue.

The monastery bowl
glows with light
the angel pours upon the world.
Sing, Caedmon, sing. No whales
nor frost nor sun nor moon
nor heat to bless the Lord with
Sidrach-song.

Past God's big hand the light
falls down until the firmament
is wet with light and every
uncreated bird is wakened
to his heritage of dawns.

Drawing in colored inks,
Caedmon Ms. Junius XI Bodleian Library

EACH DAY

Her face thins almost
as we watch. Bones

seem larger—grating
on pillow and sheet

like shells on a hedge
of shore. We speak

more simply in her presence:
a primer of nouns

and verbs. She lets go
of life gently. We

receive from her hands
the victory of belief,

learning the meaning of
our lives from our grief.

Boynton Merrill, Jr.

THE MULE

Row after row
Corn leaves broke their spines
On my shoulders.

I leaned my life
Against harness.
I drew it through
Fields, down trails,
In timbered darkness.

The corn leaves
Then turned brown.
I dragged the logs away
On washed-out roads,
And I became afraid.
I tried the ground for failure
With my feet.
I did not trust
The very earth
Which kept me from falling.

I found no treachery,
No pitfall; just sun, time,
Dust, and at last the night.

Thomas Merton

THE READER

Lord, when the clock strikes
Telling the time with cold tin
And I sit hooded in this lectern

Waiting for the monks to come,
I see the red cheeses, and bowls
All smile with milk in ranks upon their tables.

Light fills my proper globe
(I have won light to read by
With a little, tinkling chain)

And the monks come down the cloister
With robes as voluble as water.
I do not see them but I hear their waves.

It is winter, and my hands prepare
To turn the pages of the saints:
And to the trees Thy moon has frozen on the windows
My tongue shall sing Thy Scripture.

Then the monks pause upon the step
(With me here in this lectern
And Thee there on Thy crucifix)
And gather little pearls of water on their fingers' ends
Smaller than this my psalm.

Vassar Miller

A BIRD IN THE HAND

I do not feel the peace of the saints,
light fusing with darkness,
passing all understanding.

Nor yet the peace of the dead, who have drifted
beyond stir and stillness,
nothing to understand.

Mine, the catching of breath after pain,
the peace of those who have
almost died and still live.

I pray that the peace of God fall upon me;
the dead's comes unprayed;
but, for now, this suffices.

Harry Morris

BECAUSE THOU DID'ST GIVE

Out of the garden comes the tree
And in the tree bright angel,
Out of the tree, vast mystery:
Crib-tree and dark evangel.

MAINE LAKE AT NIGHT

Crossing this lake at night in a shell canoe
Is like blind flight in a wingless training plane.
The stars provide no compass; every slap
Of water bears an equal quadrant angle
To Antares or the shore. The wooded clumps,
Massive and dark, are lost; the loon scream mocks
A human cry of drowning on the water,
And a cow moose tries her frantic rage
Upon the wolves that shuffle for her calf.

WHERE LIE ALL THE SLAIN

I saw a trash-pit, filled and topped with earth;
Large jagged fragments of stone, to contrive
Some firmness, were but half buried by the live
Brown soil. The underbrush and the shrub rebirth
Led down the fertile sides; and I, in dark
Unwound a thread among the labyrinths
Of protruding shapes which seemed like broken plinths.

And bending close, I saw the chisel mark:
Died 1910; and all about was dread,
And all around the slabs gave up the dead.
How had it come about? these monuments,
Themselves interred upon these tenements,
As yet not stones of crumbled age, but vain
And young in death?
                      And where lie all the slain?

Edwin Muir

THE ANIMALS

They do not live in the world,
Are not in time and space.
From birth to death hurled
No word do they have, not one
To plant a foot upon,
Were never in any place.

For with names the world was called
Out of the empty air,
With names was built and walled,
Line and circle and square,
Dust and emerald;
Snatched from deceiving death

By the articulate breath.
But these have never trod
Twice the familiar track,
Never never turned back
Into the memoried day.
All is new and near
In the unchanging Here
Of the fifth great day of God,
That shall remain the same,

Never shall pass away.
On the sixth day we came.

THE ANNUNCIATION

The angel and the girl are met.
Earth was the only meeting place.
For the embodied never yet
Travelled beyond the shore of space.
The eternal spirits in freedom go.

See, they have come together, see,
While the destroying minutes flow,
Each reflects the other's face
Till heaven in hers and earth in his
Shine steady there. He's come to her
From far beyond the farthest star,
Feathered through time. Immediacy
Of strangest strangeness is the bliss
That from their limbs all movement takes.
Yet the increasing rapture brings
So great a wonder that it makes
Each feather tremble on his wings.

Outside the window footsteps fall
Into the ordinary day
And with the sun along the wall
Pursue their unreturning way
That was ordained in eternity.
Sound's perpetual roundabout
Rolls its numbered octaves out
And hoarsely grinds its battered tune.

But through the endless afternoon
These neither speak nor movement make,
But stare into their deepening trance
As if their gaze would never break.

Howard Nemerov

A CABINET OF SEEDS DISPLAYED

These are the original monies of the earth,
In which invested, as the spark in fire,
They will produce a green wealth toppling tall,
A trick they do by dying, by decay,
In burial becoming each his kind
To rise in glory and be magnified
A million times above the obscure grave.

Reader, these samples are exhibited
For contemplation, locked in potency
And kept from act for reverence's sake.
May they remind us while we live on earth
That all economies are primitive;
And by their reservations may they teach
Our governors, who speak of husbandry
And think the hurricane, where power lies.

TRANSLATION

Anima quodammodo omnia,
How lovely and exact the fit between
The language and the thing it means to say.
In English all but the sense evaporates:
The soul is in a manner all there is.
What's that but a poor thin mingy thing
Fit for the brain alone? Where is that world,
Where did it go, in which they said those things

And sang those things in their high halls of stone?
Vanished utterly, and we have instead
The world is everything that is the case,
That's flat enough to satisfy no one
After the lonely longings of plainsong:
In paradisum deducant te angeli,
What's that in other syllables and modes,
Now angels lead thee into paradise?
It still may draw a tremor and a tear
Sometimes, if only for its being gone,
That untranslatable, translated world
Of the Lady and the singers and the dead.

Frank O'Hara

TO THE HARBORMASTER

I wanted to be sure to reach you;
though my ship was on the way it got caught
in some moorings. I am always tying up
and then deciding to depart. In storms and
at sunset, with the metallic coils of the tide
around my fathomless arms, I am unable
to understand the forms of my vanity
or I am hard alee with my Polish rudder
in my hand and the sun sinking. To
you I offer my hull and the tattered cordage
of my will. The terrible channels where
the wind drives me against the brown lips
of the reeds are not all behind me. Yet
I trust the sanity of my vessel; and
if it sinks, it may well be in answer
to the reasoning of the eternal voices,
the waves which have kept me from reaching you.

Elder Olson

REFLECTIONS ON MIRRORS
For Richard McKeon

I

A mirror copies everything it sees
And only thus can be the thing it is.

One mirror mirrors only what it can.
Two mirrors can reflect infinity.

A broken mirror becomes many mirrors.
Broken, it mirrors what it could not, whole.

A mirror hanging in an empty house
Reflects that emptiness, and is not empty.

A mirror suspended in the absolute Void
Would be filled with the reflection of that Void.

A mirror left in darkness reflects darkness;
Truth, then, is something other than the light.

II

Cloud-like, the seasons pass, reflected here.
This, reflecting them, is of no season.

The roaring world is silent in the mirror;
Things move in the mirror; it is motionless.

All that ranting drama become dumbshow,
Gesticulation of phantoms; nothing more.

III

To see in silence all that passes by,
And when it goes, dismiss all memory of it;

Reflect at once the fire and the ice,
At once the land, the sea; be both, and neither;

To be a surface, yet contain a depth;
Bounded by dimensions, yet unbounded;

The Place of Forms: one Form, all forms, none;
Paradox of the Many made the One;

Pure act of contemplation, of the actual only,
The single act accomplished without motion.

IV

How clear, how softly luminous its world.
To seek to enter is to shatter it.

Its only secrets candor and serenity,
Learned only by the candid and serene:

Sky-colored lakes, glazed streams, polished ice,
Prisms of rain; star-imprisoning dews,

The tranquil sea; diamond; diamond tears;
The mirroring eyes; the mirror of the mind.

Linda Pastan

ASPECTS OF EVE

To have been one
of many ribs
and to be chosen.
To grow into something
quite different
knocking finally
as a bone knocks
on the closed gates of the garden—
which unexpectedly
open.

DAVID

this one, said the sculptor, is the last of the biblical figures

The last of the biblical figures
is David, carved
from the trunk of an ash.
If we place him in our rooms
he will make music.
If we burn him in our stoves
he will give heat.
The ash comes to flower
again, each leaf
is a note the harp plays.
And as the sap rises
the word lifts

to the mouth to be spoken.
David.
The knots of your tree
break the teeth of our saws.
The book will outlast
even its pages.

Paul Ramsey

THE ANGELS

The angels take approaches. Some enter by root
And others cloud-following, cloud-brightening, come.
Some in street clothes walk a gloomy one or two miles
And do not enter conversations, but watch trees,
City soot, gables that are cracked with many snows,
And limp into a bar, and hear each word which speaks
Even with broken love to cheer them as they turn,
And look into the empty mirrors, and depart.
And there are lovely angels which touch young faces;
These are as necessary to us as breathing
And words rarely capture the approach of their wings.
And there are great angels on great hills when wars come
Who know so much about justice they grow weary
But hold their beautiful adamant swords steady
And have such endurance we have great need of them.
And there are others who can do nothing but stand
In a given place and enter water and trees,
Wooden benches, a turn of weed-fixed light, a stone
White barred with grey and singular in its standing.
At certain hours one can view their plain, their sacred
Countenances. These are the ones whom I know best,
My companions, my intercessors, and my friends.

THE HOURS
For Roland D. Carter

The book of hours
Has a cipher
To be broken.

The illuminations
In the margins
Touch its music.

Rains wash
Not far
Away.

The book of hours
Turns its pages
On our coaxing.

A dancer enters.
He will bow
And dance away.

An hour readies
In the silence
We have misspoken.

A hand has touched
The pages
Of the day.

IMAGES FOR THE GOSPEL OF CHRIST

If one revolves a vine-enamored thumb
Against the grape, a smoothness comes of it.

The wine is after, decorously dark,
And after after, madnesses, the stark
Ingraining seizures that have left men dumb
Or speaking tongues which have a share of wit
Akin to rage, or rage's counterfeit.

Or it is like a sea. No plank to shore
Men up, no compass there, a place to swim
Where strong waves range and indolently flash.
Or like a coal of fire. Or like a gash
Still living, winking out inclement gore
That vanishes where mossy earth grows dim
And slow roots alter what they take of Him.

Or like the quiet music of our need,
Or like a thawing brook whose waters run
Silver and slow. Or like a pearl of price
That pays for all we are and shall suffice
At the far edge of death. Or like a seed
That grows as silently as it is sown.
Or like a walk on Sunday in the sun.

Belle Randall

CITY HALL

City Hall, five a.m.
granite steps, thumb-smudged doors,
grimy in the grim gray light
as Crime Lab photographs
enlarged in grainy black and white.

PLAYING AT CARDS

It's not as if we never played at cards—
Canasta, rummy, 21—
Ours is a standard deck;
                    808
                Bicycle
            Rider Back
"Well, look at this," says Mrs. Woo,
Showing me the back of one:

Approaching from a universe
More old and intricate than lace
An angel on a bicycle
Lends skill and chance the mark of grace.

She holds it in the light a while,
Lost deep inside that dark design
Whereby things secular become
Conveyances of things divine.

I dream: a woman standing at her mirror
Is saying, "Sometimes when I talk to you
I get the feeling it is I
   Am playing solitaire."

Behind her in the darkened room, a man
Answers as he lays the cards face down.
"How come you never look at things
The other way around?"

The evening darkens. In the lobby of
The Brown Hotel in Chinatown
Cigars are lit. A television glows.
Beside a dusty palm, old men

With freckle-spattered fingers doze.
Sifting through our talk, the sound
Of laughter and of gangster shows
Is comforting as falling rain.

Listening, one thinks of how
As faces turn toward lighted screens
In darkened rooms on upper floors,
The populations of our dreams

Divide and multiply like cells
Into a myriad of tiny selves
Whose blue light spills, whose music swells
Down hallways in a hundred brown hotels.

Julia Randall

MIRACLES

I said to the stream, Be still, and it was still.
I walked across the water like a fool.
Such ease—you'd think a man had never tried
The simple miracles, but lived and died
Sweating at wood and steel: chop, forge, bend, bind,
Get up the armory, don't trust humankind,
They were damned from the start.

                  I said to the mineral hill,
Lie down, and the hanging rocks and the canyons fell
As soft as smoke. It was quiet. I called out
Some friends to look. For a while they walked about
Uncomfortably, I thought, and one picked up
A fragment for the Museum. Envy? Fear?
I don't know what. I kept on all that year.
Wherever I went, the trees bowed down; the fruit
Rolled like obedient coins to my feet,
And so on. Late one night I tried to command—
How shall I say?—my holy spell to end,
Break, blast, unmagic me here in the dark
Tower I'd built. I wanted a horn to knock
The cullis in, and the crazy ditch to rise.
Oh god, for the need of nails, for the wild eyes
Of Noah with creation in his hold
Stampeding. But I'd sold
My Ararat for meadows. Oh, the flowers!
Too deep, too deep.
I said, accept my tears.

I. A. Richards

END OF A COURSE
In Memory of Theodore Spencer:
4 July 1902—18 January 1949

He and I,
Giving Humanities I together,
Iliad, Old Testament, Phaedo . . . I,
New Testament, Paradiso, Hamlet . . . he,
Strolled to my room through the open weather.
Full January thaw. Examination weighed,
He turned to go: 'The readiness is all!'
Said to the Calendar on the wall,
Stooping to glance at it to see
The date in Spring when we'd be free.
'Earlier than ever!' Rubbing his hands in glee,
Leapt down my steps into the sun.

All done.
He crossed the Yard, waved to a friend,
Looked up a book, then took
A taxi-ride that had no end.

NOTHING AT ALL
For Roman Jakobsen

Nothing at all can I guess,
    For all I do,
Of what in me says, YES,

Letting What's On go through
Or else says, NO.

Within my inmost mind
It runs the Show,
Leaving me resigned
Nothing at all to know;
Yet it writes this too:
That Who-cares-What
Which rules me so,
Lets me or not.
And is the You
It's speaking to.

TRINITY BRETHREN ATTEND

There was a young fellow went by:
Alight his eye
And his step was free.
But what could he see?
What could he be?
Ah, me!

Here's an old buffer drawn near:
Oh, dear,
Do what he will
He sees less still!

In between;
The man,
Firm and cool:
Their measure and their mean:
Green
And a fool.

Any day now
When all is said and done
The three
Will be
One
With Nineveh
And Tyre and Babylon;
As—in a different way,
But who knows how?—
They
Under their
Self-same star
Were
And are.

Edouard Roditi

THE NIGHT PRAYER OF GLÜCKEL OF HAMELN

Lord, Thou who art like the sea,
Only more vast, more formless,
Halcyonlike have I built my nest on Thee
Spread out all around me as far as I could see.

The year, like myself, grows old and grey,
Cold in its extremities in winter, awaits
The new year that will close its frozen eyes
When the last night has left it sightless, breathless.

Lord, I myself wait that this long
Year of life should draw to its close, that my children
Should remember me rich in crops, having stored
Enough to feed them and their children throughout

Lean years to come. The week begins
Heavy with child, with the thought of Thee
Conceived on Thy Sabbath. My worldly
Cares stifle this child, still-born when Thy seventh

Day returns with respite for the weary mother.
Around me the night is curled like a shell
Still loud with rumor of the stormy day,
Reminding me of yesterday, preparing me for

Tomorrow. My pledges must be redeemed. Diamonds
Are up: the stillness of these stones

Contrasts so strangely with our times
When men lose faith in other wares.

In days of bad faith have I given
Thee credit, been just with my debtors
Even as Thou hast promised justice
To all who are bound by lease of life

To Thy statutes. Lord, must I give
The fruit of my body that my soul be saved,
Or save this fruit from the wrath to come
At the cost of my soul? I have toiled, amassed

Great wealth, earned hard words from my debtors
And harder from those who work in my factories.
Must my children toil as I have toiled, is there
No respite for my race in the years to come?
Lord, let them sleep, let their childish minds
Not know the fear of the unknown years,
Of accounts to be rendered to man and to Thee
On the day of reckoning which stands in my books

And Thy Book. On Thy night sky are scrawled
The balanced calculations of Thy worlds,
Reminding me of the daily balance to be kept
Between being and no-being, debit and credit,

That in my limited world below
I may keep a precarious poise reflecting
From day to day the vast harmony
Of Thy stars that guide me on Time's high seas.

Theodore Roethke

THE WAKING

I wake to sleep, and take my waking slow.
I feel my fate is what I cannot fear.
I learn by going where I have to go.

We think by feeling. What is there to know?
I hear my being dance from ear to ear.
I wake to sleep, and take my waking slow.

Of those so close beside me, which are you?
God bless the Ground! I shall walk softly there,
And learn by going where I have to go.

Light takes the Tree; but who can tell us how?
The lowly worm climbs up a winding stair;
I wake to sleep, and take my waking slow.

Great Nature has another thing to do
To you and me; so take the lively air,
And, lovely, learn by going where to go.

This shaking keeps me steady. I should know.
What falls away is always. And is near.
I wake to sleep, and take my waking slow.
I learn by going where I have to go.

THE DECISION

I

What shakes the eye but the invisible?
Running from God's the longest race of all.
A bird kept haunting me when I was young—
The phoebe's slow retreating from its song,
Nor could I put that sound out of my mind,
The sleepy sound of leaves in a light wind.

II

Rising or falling's all one discipline!
The line of my horizon's growing thin!
Which is the way? I cry to the dread black,
The shifting shade, the cinders at my back.
Which is the way? I ask, and turn to go,
As a man turns to face on-coming snow.

David Rosenberg

A FOUNTAIN FROM WILDERNESS STONE
(The Book of Psalms and the Haggadah)

When Israel came out of Egypt
like a child suddenly free
from a people of strange speech

Judah became a home
for the Children of Israel
as they became a Sanctuary

for the God of their fathers—
the House of Israel
were brought into the open

and as the Sea saw them coming
it ran from the sight
the Jordan stopped dead in its tracks

mountains leaped like frightened rams
hills were a scattering flock
of lambs

What was so alarming, Sea?
Jordan, what vision
drained your strength away?

Mountains, why did you quake
like fearful rams?
Hills, why did you jump like lambs?

All earth, tremble
in the presence
of your maker

it was the God of Jacob
and he is here
all around you

a sudden pool of water
from a desert rock
a fountain from wilderness stone—

life from a heart of stone
and from bitter tears
a sweet land.

(Psalm 114)

from *TO PUT YOUR MOUTH TO DUST*
(The Book of Lamentations)

Aleph

It is I who have seen
with just a man's eyes

suffering beyond the power of men
to know is there

a wrath so deep
we are struck dumb

and we are sheep
seized by animal terror

defenseless before a world unleashed
from anything human

we have seen its frenzy raised like an arm
but we feel our shepherd's blow

Bet

He has led me into darkness
a valley no light can reach

nothing to illumine the smallest step I take
though I follow what he alone may teach

he has turned against me
with the arm that pointed my way

it is I alone who felt his hand
all sleepless night and day again

he reduced me to skin and bones
my skin was paper for his heavy hand

I was under siege
I was herded into ghettoes

Ghimel

My mind was utterly stranded
surrounded by seas of poverty

he let me sit in the dark
until I could not think

I was sealed up in a tomb
with the ancient dead

I was fenced in like sheep
I was locked in an empty room

I was bound in chains
I could not turn around

I could not stand up to pray
he had turned away

Dalet

I would cry after him for help
my throat was dry as clay

all my hopes came to roadblocks
all my dreams to barbed wire

inside myself I was exposed in a desert
all my ways arrived at despair

he was a scorpion in my path
a lion crouching in the brush

he had become my nightmare
a mad bear in my tracks

a cancer waiting inside me
a fear of being torn to pieces

*   *   *   *

Zayen

I forgot what goodness means
shalom meant nothing to me

and I thought: my spirit is dead
hope in God is beyond me

I was broken down, mumbling
I was shattered by anxiety

the more I thought about my suffering—
remembering the agony of my losses—

the more I tasted wormwood
turning to poison within me

and now, still, I remember everything
my soul staggers into exile:

Het

Memory the weight on my back
and deep in my breast every crushing detail

I cannot close my eyes before it
I cannot rise from my bed

and yet I do each day
and I rouse my heart

that the memory itself so vividly lives
awakens a deathless hope

loving-kindness like air
cannot be used up

though I breathe heavily, locked in a room
beyond the wall a wind blows freely

*   *   *   *

Kaph

How good to be desolate and alone
because the Lord does not reject forever

after the intensity of anger
mercy returns in a firm embrace

because his love lasts forever
beyond anything we can know

no matter how far away
he does not abandon his creation

we were not tormented lightly
yet nothing in him desired suffering

he didn't desire to make us earth's prisoners
returning to the dust at our feet

*   *   *   *

Samech

Where the will and faith turn bitter
repent that loss, return to him

take your heart in your hands
lift it high

sweetness flows from a broken heart
to heaven

we have hurt and destroyed
in self-righteous ignorance

Lord, we were lost in clouds of our own making
you could not forgive this

you knocked us down
you exposed us to your anger

*   *   *   *

Shin

You gave me the right to be myself
and you've seen men take it away

you've seen the hands across my mouth
Lord, speak for me and clear my name

even words have been subverted
I was brought to the bar of injustice

you saw their barbarous vengeance
you saw their final solution

my life was a living death
I was butchered for you

my death was the solution to all their problems
all their imagination was brought to my dying

*

For the hands they raise to slaughter us
with your hand, Lord, strike them deeply within

let their pride be the poison they swallow
their hearts are stones, their minds tombstones

etched there forever let all their words mock them
with their bloody thoughts spilling into silent dust.
*

(Chapter 3)

Ernest Sandeen

A PLAINT OF FLOWERS

Although, those years, we squandered
grief upon our dead
as rich and wild as blood,
time was the healthy animal

infecting our every breath.
But now, my oldest friend,
expect from me no sorrow
beyond this formal plaint of flowers.

I have no heartbeat moment
left to lavish on any
death but mine. My pride
lies withered here like yours, I feel

your pockets for the penny
you leave behind unspent.
Yet somewhere in this mortician's
scene your death and mine together,

should, like strong young men, stand weeping.

THEY ARE WICKED

They are wicked, I'm sure of that,
but they are gentle. Some of them
sit with me every day in my boat
holding their rods over the side.

They never show me what they pull
up from the deep dark under us
although I ask them many clever
questions. Then they beach my boat
on the dry sand and climb out.

No, no, they murmur, please
don't get up. And they walk away.

THE WAY DOWN

She was able to kill herself.
She had the strength
and she dared.
But then her hands being dead
could not bury her.
That harder thing to do
she left to us.
It's what we're doing here
this morning.
We may never get it done.

Karl Shapiro

from *ADAM AND EVE*

I

The Sickness of Adam

In the beginning, at every step, he turned
As if by instinct to the East to praise
The nature of things. Now every path was learned
He lost the lifted, almost flower-like gaze

Of a temple dancer. He began to walk
Slowly, like one accustomed to be alone.
He found himself lost in the field of talk;
Thinking became a garden of its own.

In it were new things: words he had never said,
Beasts he had never seen and knew were not
In the true garden, terrors, and tears shed
Under a tree by him, for some new thought.

And the first anger. Once he flung a staff
At softly coupling sheep and struck the ram.
It broke away. And God heard Adam laugh
And for his laughter made the creature lame.

And wanderlust. He stood upon the Wall
To search the unfinished countries lying wide
And waste, where not a living thing could crawl,
And yet he would descend, as if to hide.

His thought drew down the guardian at the gate,
To whom man said, 'What danger am I in?'
And the angel, hurt in spirit, seemed to hate
The wingless thing that worried after sin,

For it said nothing but marvelously unfurled
Its wings and arched them shimmering overhead,
Which must have been the signal from the world
That the first season of our life was dead.

Adam fell down with labor in his bones,
And God approached him in the cool of day
And said, 'This sickness in your skeleton
Is longing. I will remove it from your clay.'

He said also, 'I made you strike the sheep.'
It began to rain and God sat down beside
The sinking man. When he was fast asleep
He wet his right hand deep in Adam's side

And drew the graceful rib out of his breast.
Far off, the latent streams began to flow
And birds flew out of Paradise to nest
On earth. Sadly the angel watched them go.

VII

Exile

The one who gave the warning with his wings,
Still doubting them, held out the sword of flame
Against the Tree of Whiteness as they came
Angrily, slowly by, like exiled kings,

And watched them at the broken-open gate
Stare in the distance long and overlong,

And then, like peasants, pitiful and strong,
Take the first step toward earth and hesitate.

For Adam raised his head and called aloud,
'My Father, who has made the garden pall,
Giving me all things and then taking all,
Who with your opposite nature has endowed

Woman, give us your hand for our descent.
Needing us greatly, even in our disgrace,
Guide us, for gladly do we leave this place
For our own land and wished-for banishment.'

But woman prayed, 'Guide us to Paradise.'
Around them slunk the uneasy animals,
Strangely excited, uttering coughs and growls,
And bounded down into the wild abyss.

And overhead the last migrating birds,
Then empty sky. And when the two had gone
A slow half-dozen steps across the stone,
The angel came and stood among the shards

And called them, as though joyously, by name.
They turned in dark amazement and beheld
Eden ablaze with fires of red and gold,
The garden dressed for dying in cold flame,

And it was autumn, and the present world.

Robert B. Shaw

GRASS WIDOWS

Your dandelions dotting half
a casual summer lawn
mature to let their fertile chaff
uncouple and be gone;

a chance breeze or a child's puff
yellow-buttons leagues of green.
Call it a Life Force? Call it fluff.
The tatty clusters mean

whatever you may wish them to,
breathing abroad the seed
that's found a go-between in you.
Insouciantly weed,

these have neither toiled nor spun:
like their lily neighbor
lean at ease in rain and sun,
blest for lack of labor.

And labor's lost. Grass goes unmown.
You watch them grow up gold
and thick as midnight stars were shown
to Abraham who was old.

Myra Sklarew

HOLOCAUST

Could you register birds
migrating
Could you count them all
or ants in the ant hill
or bees returning to the hive
or the dead rocking in the earth

INSTRUCTIONS FOR ELIJAH

If you mean to keep this appointment
you must come tonight.
There will be no further notice.
The door will be opened,
the cup filled,
the chair left empty.

In the vineyard
we have slaughtered the children
and set them into the presses
for ritual wine.
You must take your place
among us.
The night is long.
The dough baking
takes on the landscape
of the desert.

They say we must warm ourselves
in your fiery ascent.

We have also killed a man,
set him into a cross of wood,
a dense wood whose petals
are notched and stained.
They say we have brought down
a long night upon ourselves.

NINTH OF AV

These are the days whose fingers
are divided like the horns

of a she-goat or the horns of a ram;
when the marble hands of old men

tremble in the graveyard,
making the priestly blessing

under a silken shawl, the totem
rising from between their parted fingers.

Days bound in torn cloth
go like feet in a night march.

The feet of the stolen days mark time
all night against the wooden sides

of a box where they will go
to ash, to dust.

TEACHING THE CHILDREN

Children,
today we offer you
the holocaust.

Here are the bodies here
the bunkers here the young
who were the guards.

We offer to you
dear children
this package.

It may go off
in your hands if
you open it hastily

or later
if you set it aside.

Paul Smyth

from A *FRAME FOR THE ANGELS*

39.

The Spring that I was six I found in the woods
Far in back of our house a little dump,
A pile of rusty cans, bottles, and one

Treasure: an Underwood typewriter, ancient, rusty,
Rusted solid in fact. But the black keys
Had not rusted, the bakelite or whatever it was

Had held the letters legible there in the woods,
And I, who knew the alphabet, had stared
Dumbfounded at that mysterious order. *No wonder,*

*No wonder they threw it out, the letters are all
Mixed up.* I hunted for A and B and C
And through to Z, touching them one by one.

I remained dumbfounded long after I'd asked
And learned the reason for that disorder. The logic
I lacked there in the woods was, all along,

Right in the very structure of my hands.

Anne Stanford

from *THE COVENANT OF GRACE*
a poem about Anne Hutchinson

Brother Symmes conversed with her on the ship
A woman of strange opinions, he said of her.
And she spoke of revelations.
But we women came to love her.

Ever ready to come to us in illness
With herbs and sweet words.
How many children she led into the world!
In birth and death, giving the milk of her words.

Whoever confesses the son of God
God dwells in him and he in God.
He fills my heart with grace
I and my beloved are one.

And to those of us who on the Sabbath
Lay ill or were unclean, lest we miss the preaching
She held for us a meeting
And opened up the words of the preacher.

Twenty, fifty, eighty we came
To hear her speak of love
And the work of grace in our hearts.
We found love in that pious house.

And the men, hearing of it
Came too, in from the country

In from the fields and the shops.
She spoke to us of salvation.

> O the depths of God's grace
> The heights of his salvation
> The overflowing of his goodness
> The mystery of his Covenant.

> He who hung the stars as lamps
> Cast out chaos, lit the sun,
> And flung forth meadows and fields.
> Does he not care for us?

> He gave us the Son
> And the Spirit to dwell in us
> Christ freely gives saving faith
> And the Spirit speaks to us.

*

She stood at the table before the governor
In the meeting-house at Newtown.
Behind him, magistrates, deputies,
None of them looked kindly on her.

See the impudent boldness of a proud dame.
Look at her fierce speech and countenance!
She is no Daniel, but the lions set loose.

The trial went forward
The days of hurled opinions
The probing of the ministers
Her telling of revelation
Her imprisonment in a private house.

> *I think the Soule be nothing but Light.*

Then came the Admonishing.
Her friend, her teacher, standing at the lectern
His words struck deep in her heart
As they had on a day in Saint Botolph's.

． ． ． ．

And the voice of her enemy rose in the meeting-house:
I pronounce you worthy to be cast out
And I cast you out. In the name of Christ
I deliver you up to Satan.
I account you from this time a heathen
I command you as a leper to draw out of the congregation.

       The Lord judgeth not as man judgeth
       Better to be cast out
       Than to deny Christ.

*

Away from the meeting-house, the cluster
Of houses, the fort on the hill,
Across the river singing sweetly
The creak of the harness, the road through the meadows

In rainy April into the forest
Across the swelling streams to Rhode Island
With Francis, Bridget, Sam, young Anne
Maria, Kate, young Will, Zuryell, and Susan.

And from Providence to Aquidneck
And even there pursued
Thence to Long Island, to fall at last
Still praising God, under the arrows at Pelham.

Timothy Steele

ONE MORNING

One morning, rubbing clear the windowpane,
He grows coherent. The dark aimless rain

Becomes, abruptly, perfect thought; the jeans
Draped from the chair, that vase, the magazines

Scattered on his desk seem to draw within
Some final syllable. And who he's been,

Or what, no longer counts. The hours dispose
The silence and the light, advance and close

Into his will alone. Force? Harmony?
It is his time, whose coming even he

Could never quite imagine—simple, clear,
And endlessly complete. Right now. Right here.

RURAL COLLOQUY WITH A PAINTER

By noon, as I recall, the sky was clear,
The meadow drying in the wind and sun.
And the dark boughs of a hillside spruce in motion,
We sat on your porch drinking Hires Root Beer
As you expatiated on the notion—
Your cherished old Whiteheadean ideal—
That form and movement are, or can be, one.

From a black granite shelf, your spaniel watched
Crows angle toward the wood. Serene, you praised
Eakins and Hopper—your hands giving shape
To what you said: *The logical escape*
From all the self's excesses is the real.
And then with a mock flourishing, you raised
Your glass and, in a long gulp, downed your drink.

And I, although not quite convinced, could think
That those wildflowers whose names I'd never know,
The spruce, the hillside, and the field below
Would offer their concurrence if they could.
And then, if form and movement were not one,
It hardly mattered much there in the sun.
I think that Whitehead might have understood.

Francis Sullivan

PRAYER

You may be right, divinity,
everything is nothing alongside You.
Love may be plucks on strings;
the hand, the mime of true music.

You will crush me, if so.

There are barer lands than mine,
without water.
The corn there is starveling.
The city, elsewhere than here, smacks
shells between two bricks,
as with meatless walnuts.

Some mornings are pregnant.

I want them with an earthly hunger.

Some are polished sea shells, nautilus,
or fragments of abalone. They plumb me
with an earthly joy I am lost in.

There are bare leaves elsewhere.
They have no memories of times together,
evenings in the smell of grapes,
or with carved wood of You splitting
at the cheekbones with age,
or in birth or death.

I want You with an earthly hunger.

Elsewhere, there are hungers greater.

STILL LIFE

white and red
camellias
rot in a bowl,
as fruit,
but what they were
when ripe
and open
in clear water
cannot be annulled
even by their own
decay,
when they bend
too far back
and let go their hold
on their own pollen,
gold crumbs
stuck to small fingers
held up for
looks and licks
in the center of
a revelation of
what cannot be
annulled by rot,
if it has happened
once in a bowl
of clear water,
however soon
we put them in
the trash
to be a death

new camellias
cannot,
in their turn,
annul.

R.S. *Thomas*

JUDGMENT DAY

Yes, that's how I was,
I know that face,
That bony figure
Without grace
Of flesh or limb;
In health happy,
Careless of the claim
Of the world's sick
Or the world's poor;
In pain craven—
Lord, breathe once more
On that sad mirror,
Let me be lost
In mist for ever
Rather than own
Such bleak reflections.
Let me go back
On my two knees
Slowly to undo
The knot of life
That was tied there.

Robert Wallace

A PROBLEM IN HISTORY

At morning light the ark lay grounded fast
On top of Ararat; and Noah sent out
The raven flapping on jet-fingered wings
Unreturning; and thrice to look about
Sent the timid dove, that returned at last
Fluttering an olive bough. The robin sings

On the spattered rail and the sun shines
On the steaming earth, that like a bog stank
Greening at the clear blue sky. Asses bray
From the hold, the animals come down the plank
By twos and twos, in awkward-footed lines
Sniffing, while hawks and songbirds spray

Into the new air. Forgetful of the flood,
In a busy hour all are debarked and gone
Down from Ararat. By sunfall the voices
Of their going have vanished. The ark alone
Centers their outward footprints in the mud,
Settles through the night with creaking noises

Wearied with its long journey. In that repose
New suns will wreathe it with green-ivy vines,
Shade it with growing oaks and bushes round
There on the world's top, till it rots with rains
And snows and suns of time. And no one knows
What green the unreturning raven found.

Robert Penn Warren

GOLD GLADE

Wandering, in autum, the woods of boyhood,
Where cedar, black, thick, rode the ridge,
Heart aimless as rifle, boy-blankness of mood,
I came where the ridge broke, and a great ledge,
Limestone, set my toe high as treetops by the dark edge

Of a gorge, and water hid, grudging and grumbling,
And I saw, in my mind's eye, foam white on
Wet stone, stone wet-black, white water tumbling,
And so went down, and with some fright on
Slick boulders, crossed over. The gorge-depth drew night on,

But high over high rock and leaf-lacing, the sky
Showed yet bright, and declivity wooed
My foot by the quietening stream, and so I
Went on, in quiet, through the beech wood:
There, in gold light, where the glade gave, it stood.

The glade was geometric, circular, gold,
No brush or weed breaking that bright gold of leaf-fall.
In the center it stood, absolute and bold
Beyond any heart-hurt, or eye's grief-fall.
Gold-massy in air, it stood in gold light-fall,

No breathing of air, no leaf now gold-falling,
No tooth-stitch of squirrel, or any far fox-bark,
No woodpecker coding, or late jay calling.

Silence: gray-shagged, the great shagbark
Gave forth gold light. There could be no dark.

But of course dark came, and I can't recall
What county it was, for the life of me.
Montgomery, Todd, Christian—I know them all.
Was it even Kentucky or Tennessee?
Perhaps just an image that keeps haunting me.

No, no! in no mansion under earth,
Nor imagination's domain of bright air,
But solid in soil that gave it its birth,
It stands, wherever it is, but somewhere.
I shall set my foot, and go there.

Richard Wilbur

from THE MIND-READER

What should I tell them?
I have no answers. *Set your fears at rest,*
I scribble when I must. *Your paramour*
Is faithful, and your spouse is unsuspecting.
You were not seen, that day, beneath the fig-tree.
Still, be more cautious. When the time is ripe,
Expect promotion. I foresee a message
From a far person who is rich and dying.
You are admired in secret. If, in your judgement,
Profit is in it, you should take the gamble.
As for these fits of weeping, they will pass.

It makes no difference that my lies are bald
And my evasions casual. It contents them
Not to have spoken, yet to have been heard.
What more do they deserve, if I could give it,
Mute breathers as they are of selfish hopes
And small anxieties? Faith, justice, valor,
All those reputed rarities of soul
Confirmed in marble by our public statues—
You may be sure that they are rare indeed
Where the soul mopes in private, and I listen.
Sometimes I wonder if the blame is mine,
If through a sullen fault of the mind's ear
I miss a resonance in all their fretting.
Is there some huge attention, do you think
Which suffers us and is inviolate,
To which all hearts are open, which remarks

The sparrow's weighty fall, and overhears
In the worst rancor a deflected sweetness?
I should be glad to know it.

TWO VOICES IN A MEADOW

A Milkweed

Anonymous as cherubs
Over the crib of God,
White seeds are floating
Out of my burst pod.
What power had I
Before I learned to yield?
Shatter me, great wind:
I shall possess the field.

A Stone

As casual as cow-dung
Under the crib of God,
I lie where chance would have me,
Up to the ears in sod.
Why should I move? To move
Befits a light desire.
The sill of Heaven would founder,
Did such as I aspire.

THE WHALE
from the Middle English Bestiary

WHALE is the greatest beast   In all the ocean waste;
Whom if you ever espied   Sprawling upon the tide,
An isle he would seem to be   Built on the sands of the sea.

When this fierce fish would feed,   He spreads his great
                                          mouth wide,
And thence expels his breath,   The sweetest smell on earth.
The other fishes come,   Ravished by that perfume;
They dawdle within his jaws,   Unwary of the ruse.
He slams his jaw-gates then,   And drinks those fishes in . . .

This whale-fish dwells secure   Down near the ocean floor
Until that season arrives   When winter with summer strives
And storm stirs all the sea;   In such inclemency
His lair he cannot keep,   But up from the troubled deep
He rises, and lies still.   Then while the weather is ill,
Sailors driven and tossed   Who fear that they are lost,
Sighting the quiet whale,   Mistake him for an isle.
They view him with delight   And hasten with all their
                                          might

To make their vessels fast   And climb ashore at last;
With tinder, steel, and stone   They kindle a blaze thereon,
Warm them, and drink, and eat.   But, feeling the fire's
                                          heat,

The whale to sea-deep dives   And robs them of their lives.

Signification

The Devil is great in will,   With monstrous force and skill
(These powers he imparts   To witches in their arts);
He gives men hunger and thirst   And many another lust,

Drawing them by his breath,   To follow which is death . . .
Who hears the Devil's word   Will rue the day he heard;
Who ties his hopes thereto   Will plunge with him below.

William Carlos Williams

from *FOR ELEANOR AND BILL MONAHAN*

MOTHER OF GOD! Our Lady!
>   the heart
>   is an unruly Master:
Forgive us our sins
>   as we
>   forgive
those who have sinned against
>   us.
>   We submit ourselves
to Your rule
>   as the flowers in May
>   submit themselves to
>   Your Holy rule—against
that impossible spring-time
>   when men
>   shall be the flowers
spread at your feet.

AS FAR AS spring is
>   from winter
>   so are we
from you now. We have not come
>   easily
>   to your environs
but painfully
>   across sands
>   that have scored our
feet. That which we have suffered

was for us
to suffer. Now,
in the winter of the year,
the birds who know how
to escape suffering
by flight
are gone. Man alone
is that creature who
cannot escape suffering
by flight.

I DO NOT come to you
save that I confess
to being
half man and half
woman. I have seen the ivy
cling
to a piece of crumbled
wall so that
you cannot tell
by which either
stands: this is to say
if she to whom I cling
is loosened both
of us go down.

MOTHER OF GOD
I have seen you stoop
to a merest flower
and raise it
and press it to your cheek.
I could have called out
joyfully
but you were too far off.
You are a woman and
it was
a woman's gesture.

                    I declare it boldly
with my heart
            in my teeth
                        and my knees knocking
together. Yet I declare
            it, and by God's word
                        it is no lie. Make us
humble and obedient to His rule.

        from *THE GARDEN*

IT IS FAR TO ASSISI,
            but not too far:
                        Over this garden,
brooding over this garden.
            there is a kindly spirit,
                        brother to the poor
and who is poorer than he
            who is in love
                        when birds are nesting
in the spring of the year?
            They came
                        to eat from his hand
who had nothing,
            and yet
                        from his plenty
he fed them all.
            All mankind
                        grew to be his debtors,
a simple story.
            Love is in season.

AT SUCH A TIME,
            hyacinth time
                        in
the hospital garden,

                    the time
                                of the coral flowered
        and early salmon pink
                        clusters, it is
                                the time also of
        abandoned birds' nests
                        before
                                the sparrows start
                                to tear them apart
                against the advent of that bounty
                        from which
                                they will build anew.

        ALL ABOUT THEM
                        on the lawns
                                the young couples
        embrace
                        as in a tale
                                by Boccaccio

        They are careless
                        under license of the disease
                                which has restricted them
        to these grounds.
                        St. Francis forgive them
                                and all lovers
        whoever they may be.
                        They have seen
                                a great light, it
        springs from their own bawdy foreheads.
                        The light
                                is sequestered there
        by these enclosing walls.
                        They are divided
                                from their fellows.
        It is a bounty
                        from last year's nest.

St. Francis,
who befriended the wild birds,
by their aid,
those who

have nothing,
and live
by the Holy light of love

that rules,
blocking despair,
over this garden.

Yvor Winters

FOR THE OPENING OF THE WILLIAM DINSMORE BRIGGS ROOM

Because our Being grows in mind,
And evil in imperfect thought,
And passion running undefined
May ruin what the masters taught;

Within the edge of war we meet
To dedicate this room to one
Who made his wisdom more complete
Than any save the great have done.

That in this room, men yet may reach,
By labor and wit's sullen shock,
The final certitude of speech
Which Hell itself cannot unlock.

INSCRIPTION FOR A GRAVEYARD

When men are laid away,
Revolving seasons bring
New love, corrupting clay
And hearts dissevering.

Hearts that were once so fast,
Sickened with living blood,
Will rot to change at last.
The dead have hardihood.

Death is Eternity,
And all who come there stay.
For choice, now certainty.
No moment breaks away.

Amid this wilderness,
Dazed in a swarm of hours—
Birds tangled numberless!—
Archaic Summer towers.

The dead are left alone—
Theirs the intenser cost.
You followed to a stone,
And there the trail was lost.

POEM
from the Spanish of
the 16th century

Nothing move thee;
Nothing terrify thee;
Everything passes;
God never changes.
Patience be all to thee.
Who trusts in God, he
Never shall be needy.
God alone suffices.
                    —Saint Teresa

A SONG IN PASSING

Where am I now? And what
Am I to say portends?
Death is but death, and not
The most obtuse of ends.

No matter how one leans
One yet fears not to know.
God knows what all this means!
The mortal mind is slow.

Eternity is here.
There is no other place.
The only thing I fear
Is the Almighty Face.

Karol Wojtyla

MARBLE FLOOR

Our feet meet the earth in this place;
there are so many walls, so many colonnades,
yet we are not lost. If we find
meaning and oneness,
it is the floor that guides us. It joins the spaces
of this great edifice, and joins
the spaces within us,
who walk aware of our weakness and defeat.
Peter, you are the floor, that others
may walk over you (not knowing
where they go). You guide their steps
so that spaces can be one in their eyes,
and from them thought is born.
You want to serve their feet that pass
as rock serves the hooves of sheep.
The rock is a gigantic temple floor,
the cross a pasture.

SONG OF THE BRIGHTNESS OF WATER

From this depth—I came only to draw water
in a jug—so long ago, this brightness
still clings to my eyes— the perception I found,
and so much empty space, my own,
reflected in the well.

Yet it is good. I can never take all of you
into me. Stay then as mirror in the well.
Leaves and flowers remain, and each astonished gaze
brings them down
to my eyes transfixed more by light
than by sorrow.

Epigrams and
Light Verse and Kin

There's a Man Calling
Poems on Words

X. J. Kennedy

TO AN ANGRY GOD

Lend me cruel light
That, tooling over syllables I write,
I do not skim forgivingly. Not spare,
But smite.

Ernest Sandeen

POÈTE MANQUÉ

I have beaten him often, head and heel
says the Lord, and I find no sound in him,
neither the savage growl of the drum
nor the sweet clean resonance of the bell.
I never hear the sea of the seasons roll
through him, nor night and day toss and hum.
A sodden gourd, or cracked vessel, says the Lord,
he is good for nothing now but heaven or hell.

Coleman Barks

from NEW WORDS

• • • •

So it is,
riffling the S volume of OED
I come to *satispassion*.
It doesn't mean what it ought to.
Theological, for enough agony
To atone. *Deliver us not O Lord this day
from satispassion.*

• • • •

Do words protect us
with their cold light?

• • • •

mally—dotingly fond. Mally father
maketh wicked child.

mahu—a name for the devil.

• • • •

fernshaw—a thicket of ferns.
Secret places along creeks

around Chattanooga
were fernshaws, and nobody knew it.

•   •   •   •

Granted, these are for collectors,
whose lives are hidden,
As mine is to me,
faced with definitions and loose ends,
moving over a big book
like a kitchen match
feeling for a rough place.

•   •   •   •

Some words we have no record of.
Some get written down
and last for centuries
before they lose their limits
and come to mean almost anything,
nonsense words.

The best is sense and nonsense both,
child and parent,
earth and sky.

•   •   •   •

The cemetery goes on and on,
where words are buried.

•   •   •   •

Speaking dead words,
there is a confused solitude
for both of us.

Think of translating this to another language
trying to find similar terms.

Words exist somewhere
between being and not.

. . . .

A living word, though, is like the god Janus:
one face looking at meaning, the dictionary,
the other looking out the window at what is.

. . . .

Close the book
and listen.

There's a man shouting
in the middle of the street.

Get up,
for what it means.

If it's a dance,
you must dance.
If it's death,
you must die.

What a chill when it rains,
What wind.

Comes the dance
You must dance
Comes death
You can't help it

Get up.
There's a man calling
in the middle of the street.

Paul Ramsey

ON WORDS AND CONCEPTS AND THINGS

Scissors cut you? What tender ears!
How loud is *drum*? Equally, all day?
How ripe do you spell *orchard*?

Are *finger nails* or finger nails stronger?
Finger nails cannot be broken at all.

Do you see the *cat* on the mat?
Yes, or you see no cat.

Myra Sklarew

SPEECH WARTS

Fetch me a red flower from that meadow,
says Ludwig. I look at him. Which shade
of red? What species of flower? And on
what green stalk? He stares back at me.
And above all, I say to him, which meadow?
He is silent. How shall I get there with-
out losing the flower, the one he has
imagined? I take a sheet from my left
pocket which contains the shapes of all
English and American flowers. I take a
glass prism from my right pocket. Now I
march up to the nearest meadow and compare
real flowers with my chart of flower
shapes. I pass a ray of sunlight through
my prism and produce a color band which
I compare with the colors of flowers. But
the flowers in the meadow are in foreign
languages: Sprechenvorts! Gehimmelhymen-
optera! they shout at me. *Louloûdia*, they
continue to berate me, this time in Greek,
mocking my shape grilles, my color bands.
What next? I ask him. Fetch me the meadow,
he says. Be quick about it. I come back,
my arms full. I can barely walk under the
weight of sumac, wild barley, their names
heavy in Russian, Serbo-Croatian, various
Indo-European tongues. My face is a sheath
of red flowers. Not the one I had imagined,

he tells me. Not that one, he repeats.
Nowhere to be found in the vast meadow you
have brought me. I set down the meadow
before him. I take a sheet of paper from my
hip pocket. I write on it: A RED FLOWER
FROM THAT MEADOW, and I attach it to a stick
which I set upright, waving, in the center
of the meadow. That one, Ludwig whispers
gratefully. That is the one.

It Will Take Me Years, Lord:
Poems on a Number of Things

John Berryman

DREAM SONG 64

Supreme my holdings, greater yet my need,
thoughtless I go out.   Dawn.   Have I my cig's,
my flaskie O,
O crystal cock,—my kneel has gone to seed,—
and anybody's blessing? (Blast the MIGs
for making fumble so

my tardy readying.) Yes, utter' that.
Anybody's blessing?—Mr Bones,
you makes too much
démand. I might be 'fording you a hat:
it gonna rain.—I knew a one of groans
& greed & spite, of a crutch,

who thought he had, a vile night, been—well—blest.
He see someone run off. Why not Henry,
with his grasp of desire?
—Hear matters hard to manage at de best,
Mr Bones. Tween what we see, what be,
is blinds. Them blinds' on fire.

J. V. Cunningham

EPIGRAM

And what is love? Misunderstanding, pain,
Delusion, or retreat? It is in truth
Like an old brandy after a long rain,
Distinguished, and familiar, and aloof.

Fazil Hüsnü Dağlarca

HOLLOW ECHO

The shepherd plays his flute
He doesn't know
If this silence is for the sheep
Or for the hills

FIRE

When
Water forgets—
Whether darkness descends or not—
The flame opens its eyes wide

THOUGHT

I think in fours
The night thinks in sevens and nines
But God thinks
In ones

Donald Davie

from *HORAE CANONICAE*

PRIME

New every morning is the love
Our wakening and uprising prove,
Bond it in warranty a hundred proof.
Giving his thanks for roof, for bed and board,
Mr Saint Keble, meek and lowly,
White with rite, and clean with holy,
Wordplays to the morning's Lord.

Robert Francis

EXCLUSIVE BLUE

Her flowers were exclusive blue.
No other color scheme would do.

Better than God she could reject
Being a gardener more select.

Blue, blue it was against the green
With nothing *not* blue sown or seen.

Yet secretly she half-confessed
With blue she was not wholly blessed.

All blues, she found do not agree.
Blue riots in variety.

Purist-perfectionist at heart,
Her vision flew beyond her art—

Beyond her art, her touch, her power
To teach one blue to each blue flower.

O. B. Hardison, Jr.

SMALL TALK IN A GARDEN

I will admit freely that it hurt.
In fact, it hurt like hell
Although I didn't notice it at the time.

Like a damn fool I fell asleep
(If I have any fault, it's being trusting)
And along comes the famous Doctor
Penknife in hand
And starts sawing away at my rib cage.
Some day they'll catch up to him.
Lift his license.
Sue him for every cent he's got.

Anyway, I woke up and there she was,
My first experience of society.
Going out where I go in,
Going in where I go out.
There was a reason for that, as I should have realized.

I suppose I was weak from loss of blood
Or still silly from the anesthetic
Or disoriented by shock.
Whatever it was, she got to me where I live.
Remember, we hadn't grown up together,
Gotten used to each other, to the differences, as you might say.

I suppose, too, I made all sorts of silly statements.
Probably a few promises that only a fool would keep

(Not that I realized it then—
Then everything looked rosy—
But it certainly did occur to me later
That I should have kept my mouth shut).

I wasn't after much
And, frankly, she didn't have all that much to offer.
I'd watched the animals go at it.
I knew the name for it even before I'd gotten through naming
    them.
When in Rome, I say, do as the Romans.

If she were honest (which she is not) she'd confess.
She liked it just as much as I did.
She only discovered later there was a hook in it.
The good Doctor again. This time he did it without a
    penknife.
Worked it so we betrayed ourselves,
Betrayed ourselves willingly, lovingly, enjoyed it even,
Jumped singing over the cliff.

So there we were rolling around in the grass
And might be there still, for all I know,
If she hadn't gotten hungry from all that exercise,
Gone foraging all over the blooming garden,
Brought back that fruit,
Held out on me until I agreed.
Hell, at that point I would have agreed to anything.

It was then I began noticing my side was hurting.
Ached when I got up in the morning,
And, believe me, ached when I got home at night after work.

Home, that's a laugh.
Home to the usual insipid boiled cabbage,
Jello with fake whipped cream
Laced with innumerable cancer-producing chemicals.

Home to that deadly chit-chat about the boys
(Mostly Abel, a fairy if I ever saw one).

She's gone to fat now.
About as desirable as a water buffalo.
What with that and the pain in my side
I can hardly get it up any more.
None of that is as bad, however, as my uneasy feeling
That life may still hold one or two more surprises.

Donald Justice

LETHARGY

It smiles to see me
Still in my bathrobe.

It sits in my lap
And will not let me rise.

Now it is kissing my eyes.
Arms enfold me, arms

Pale with a thick down.
It seems I am falling asleep

To the sound of a story
Being read me.

This is the story.
Weeks have passed

Since first I lifted my hand
To set it down.

from THINGS

Hard, but you can polish it.
Precious, it has eyes. Can wound.
Would dance upon water. Sinks.
Stays put. Crushed, becomes a road.
          .   (STONE)

Mine to give, mine to offer
No resistance. Mine
To receive you, mine to keep
The shape of our nights.

(PILLOW)

Sister M. Madeleva, C.S.C.

from *OF MARY*

DUMB OXEN*

Mary, pray for Paris
And Bethlehem;
A dumb ox served you
In both of them.

```
              *
              O
            HOLY
            WOOD
          OF CRIB
        AND ROOD
      TODAY LET BE
              Y
              O
              U
              R
      CHRISTMAS TREE
```

*Thomas Aquinas was called "the Dumb Ox," in reference to his size and silence.

Victoria McCabe

FOR STARTERS
[from DIVORCE: A HANDBOOK FOR BEGINNERS]

Be good
in math:
know how
to add up
backbiting misdeeds,
betrayal, unjust
accusations. Multiply
by hurt feelings, lost
sleep. Subtract the myth
of Home and Family. Divide
your children, and sheets.

Phyllis McGinley

BALLADE OF LOST OBJECTS

Where are the ribbons I tie my hair with?
  Where is my lipstick? Where are my hose—
The sheer ones hoarded these weeks to wear with
  Frocks the closets do not disclose?
Perfumes, petticoats, sports chapeaux,
  The blouse Parisian, the earring Spanish—
Everything suddenly ups and goes.
  *And where in the world did the children
  vanish?*

This is the house I used to share with
  Girls in pinafores, shier than does.
I can recall how they climbed my stair with
  Gales of giggles, on their toptoes.
Last seen wearing both braids and bows
  (But looking rather Raggedy-Annish),
When they departed nobody knows—
  Where in the world did the children vanish?

Two tall strangers, now I must bear with,
  Decked in my personal furbelows,
Raiding the larder, rending the air with
  Gossip and terrible radios.
Neither my friends nor quite my foes,
  Alien, beautiful, stern, and clannish,
Here they dwell, while the wonder grows:
  where in the world did the children vanish?

Prince, I warn you, under the rose,
 Time is the thief you cannot banish.
These are my daughters, I suppose.
 But where in the world did the children vanish?

Boynton Merrill, Jr.

THE MITE

I am the least
Of living things,
A cell, a seed,
A spiral chromosome.
A tendril in the sea.

I know how mystery began,
And why the roots
Of purpose feed on pain.

N. Scott Momaday

WALK ON THE MOON
For Henry Raymont, 21 July 1969

Extend, there where you venture and come back,
The edge of Time. Be it your farthest track.
Time in that distance wanes. What is *to be,*
That present verb, there in Tranquility?

Howard Nemerov

EVE

There are no more shopping days to Christmas.
Slowly we wheel our wire cages down
And back along the fluorescent aisles,
And down and back again, prowling the maze
Of goods, by many musics played upon,
The glaze of obligation in our eyes
As we take in the dozen television sets
Tuned to the same Western, and the caged birds
No one has wanted to give, and the many
Remaining goldfish desperately marked down.

Come all ye faithful, calls the music now.
We march in time, stopping to take, put back,
And sometimes take again. We buy some rolls
Of merry wrapping paper, and push the whole
Caboodle to the counter where it's counted
And added up and put in paper bags
By the girl we pay and get the right change from
With some green stamps. She smiles, and we smile back.
A dollar bill is pinned to her left tit
Somewhere about the region of the heart.

Paul Ramsey

THREE EPIGRAMS

The Exiles

The mayor has angrily banished the seven deadly
    sins from the city.
He is proud of his achievement and the loiterers
    envy his style.
The restaurant owners prosper at the celebration
And the motel owners smile.

A Modern Theologian

True faith, he claims, has the most doubt.
Are wives most true when stepping out?

Consolations

Death does away with sickness; Hell cures chance;
And failure sets us free from sycophants.

Belle Randall

MABEL WOO

Selected and renumbered from "A Hundred Ways of
Playing Solitaire"

1

Mabel Woo,
age 49,
onetime chorus girl
(Johnny Lotus Yum-Yum Girl Review,
Chinese Capers, 1942),
stage name: Roxie Starr,
now Rexall Drugs cashier,

at age 18, elected Queen
of Chinese New Year 1938
(a yellowed clipping shows her wearing
ermine and a bathing suit,
waving from a dragon float),
set out for Hollywood to be a star—

hard, always, for an Oriental girl,
impossible during The War
("Too young for Shangri-la,
too old for *South Pacific*—
everybody took me for a Jap");

she wound up in a storefront school
teaching ballroom dance and tap;

her only speaking part—
a 1940s Charlie Chan
("A flop, but even so,"
seeing it in *TV Guide* last week,
"it lasted longer than my marriage did").
About the latter and the man—
"Ah so!" she quips, and will not speak.
And now APPEARING NIGHTLY in
         A Faded Robe
across whose purple plains
red cowboys swing gold lariats,
transistor under arm,
sleep mask perched on head,
Mabel Woo, age 49,
is on her way to bed.

She hovers in my doorway while I work,
pockets drooping like an old sow's teats
with matchbooks, Q-Tips and a few
tobacco-clung imported sweets,
not to mention Sleep-Eze
and more potent drugs
to aid her in the dark
oncoming passage into sleep.

                    2

How many midnights—"Bedtime snack?"—
She's pushed my door ajar a crack,
Inquiring if I want to share
The meager portion labeled hers
Inside our hive-top Frigidaire.

As late sometimes as one A.M.
(A book beneath her arm, an ashtray
Like an alms plate in her hand—
"I saw your light, may I come in?"),
She settles on my davenport,
Her cigarette a firefly spark,
The book unopened in her lap,
Her restless hands as thin as smoke
Rising from the red-hot ash
With which she pokes a crooked path
Through burnt-out matchsticks in a glass.

But though I guess the fear concealed
Inside these empty gestures like
A stain inside a glove,
I confess I'm filled with terror
When, stirring ashes, she begins,
"Aside from you,
                    there's nobody I love . . . "

3

Who is this Oriental pearl,
Mixed syllable of woe and rue,
Who haunts the dark side of my room?

Between the stars and me, what moon
Rising casts a pall of blue
Across these pages as I write?

Through lids so taut they seem to hurt,
Gazing, stoic, through the snow
That falls across the Late Late Show,

She mirrors my fullness in the gloom,
Cupped in dark, her oval face,
Small and empty as a spoon.

4

Water roars. Behind the wall
The next-door tenant, Mrs. Woo,
With whom I share the rumbling bowl
Of ancient toilet, chain and ball,
And "privileges" of kitchenette,
Fills the claw-foot tub we rent.

There's no way out—when Christ said Love
Thy Neighbor, this is who he meant.

John Raven

AN INCONVENIENCE

Mama,
papa,
and us
10 kids
lived in
a single room.
Once when I
got sick
and like to die,
I heard a cry
slice through the gloom
"Hotdog!
We gon have
mo room!"

David Ray

ON A FIFTEENTH-CENTURY FLEMISH ANGEL

The toe sticking out from under the hem
Of that angel's blue skirt
Shows, along with the finger raised
In no-nonsense admonishment,
That you are dealing here
With a down-to-earth angel,
An angel whose wings belong, organic
As a bird's: not like those Greco
Angels, sour-faced and grim with doubt.
The face of this particular red-haired
Angel, with blue wings and ruddy cheeks,
Holding a mace he'd use to crack
Your noggin, tingles from the chill
Of northern skies; yet those cheeks
Are luminous with the long light
Of stars. His flesh is warmed
By blood that never need be drained.

Theodore Roethke

BRING THE DAY!

1

Bees and lilies there were,
Bees and lilies there were,
Either to other,—
Which would you rather?
Bees and lilies were there.

The green grasses,—would they?
The green grasses?—
She asked her skin
To let me in:
The far leaves were for it.

Forever is easy, she said.
How many angels do you know?—
And over by Algy's
Something came by me,
It wasn't a goose,
It wasn't a poodle.

Everything's closer. Is this a cage?
The chill's gone from the moon.
Only the woods are alive.
I can't marry the dirt.

I'm a biscuit. I'm melted already.

The white weather hates me.
Why is how I like it.
I can't catch a bush.

2

The herrings are awake.
What's all the singing between?—
Is it with whispers and kissing?—
I've listened into the least waves.
The grass says what the wind says:
Begin with the rock;
End with water.

When I stand, I'm almost a tree.
Leaves, do you like me any?
A swan needs a pond.
The worm and the rose
Both love
Rain.

3

O small bird wakening,
Light as a hand among blossoms,
Hardly any old angels are around any more.
The air's quiet under the small leaves.
The dust, the long dust, stays.
The spiders sail into summer.
It's time to begin!
To begin!

Robert B. Shaw

GARGOYLE

An ornamental bung,
a dragon-dog in little,
a throat without a tongue
to sample its own spittle:

whatever I may be,
harpy or horned toad,
is all the same to me.
I labor to erode.

Good Christians, as you go
about your wonted kneeling,
be thankful you're below
a serviceable ceiling.

For centuries I've craned
my neck above your city
and never yet complained.
I am above your pity.

And you are under mine.
I dream: a day will come
of which I am the sign.
Smitten grotesquely dumb,

you'll glare to see each other sprout
tusk, antler, serrate tail,

and the appalling snout.
I trust fate not to fail,

when even today on just
and unjust Heaven can strew
that soot-laden rain I must
catch, convey and spew.

Myra Sklarew

HOW METAPHOR CAN SAVE YOUR LIFE

You are drowning.
Someone throws you an inflatable sunset
which momentarily distracts you
from the sinking ship, the cramp
in your left leg, the barracuda
who has just sidled up next to you.
You forget that you do not know
how to swim. Your thrashing about,
your simulated swimming strokes
bring out the Coast Guard.

You find a small tumor.
behind your left earlobe.
The dark cloud of cancer descends
just as the doctor tells you
you have Dutch elm disease
and need to wash more frequently
behind your ears.

You have just lost your job.
You have no money in the bank.
EAT LOVE, someone has written
on the bulletin board at the unemployment
office. A man proposes on the hard bench.
You accept and live happily
ever afterword.

You are on an airplane.
Suddenly it hits an air pocket and drops

a thousand feet into a cloud bank.
You climb out of the window. You have always
wanted to touch a cloud. You hold yourself
aloft by doing yoga. Soon your parachute
opens. You sail safely through a grove
of redwood trees, your arms full
of cumulonimbus towers from the cloud bank.
You learn that the Dow Jones is up.

WHAT IS A JEWISH POEM

Does it wear a yarmulka
and tallis?
Does it live
in the diaspora
and yearn for homeland?

Does it wave the lulav
to and fro inside
a plastic sukkah
or recite
the seven benedictions
under the chupah?

I wonder—
what is a Jewish poem?
Does it only go to synagogue
one day a year
attaching the tfillin
like a tiny black stranger
to its left arm?

Does it open
the stiff skins
of the prayerbook
to reveal the letters

like blackened platelets
twisting within?

Little yeshiva bocher,
little Jewish poem
waving your sidecurls
whispering piyyut to me
in my sleep;
little Jewish poem
in your shtreimel hat;
little grandfather,
sing to me.
Little Jewish poem,
come sing to me.

Francis J. Smith, S.J.

FIRST PRELUDE

> " . . . consider how God dwells in creatures . . . "
> *(St. Ignatius of Loyola)*

I want to go on
till the contemplation is done.
It takes a long time
to scan the curlicues
gold fish trace in play,
to say nothing of moving about
the somewhat infinite sea,
tagging leathery creatures rolling
like giant vacuum bags
with song like mountain thunder.
I have trouble defining
the melon head and cucumber snout
of a Golden Labrador I know.
I'm just beginning to mix
leaves and galaxies
and to notice the laser print
in the pursed eyes of my cat
when she is on to something.
It will take me years, Lord,
to get around to the machinery
of a human hand
able to manage needles and chopsticks.
And I must mark today
the construction of an onion.

You see, I'm getting there
but I have many more stars
to ponder in my night
than Loyola had.

Timothy Steele

A DEVOTIONAL SONNET

Lord, pity such sinners. Monday afternoon
Is not the proper time for Augustine.
My saints are porcelain, chipped clair de lune,
Books and white wine. But don't intervene:
My chastity, unwitting though it is,
Is real; nor have I worshipped bitterness.
Jobless and on the loose, my share of bliss
Is simply that I've felt what I confess.

And what absolves me? This chilled Chardonnay,
A few letters from Cambridge and Vermont,
And You, who will restrain me if I stray
Too far from love I both reject and want.
And should this be "interpreted disease,"
Yours are such sinners, such apologies.

A *Little Cage of Bone*
Poems on Death

Robert Penn Warren

from *BALLAD: BETWEEN THE BOXCARS*

I CAN'T EVEN REMEMBER THE NAME

I can't even remember the name of the one who fell
Flat on his ass, on the cinders, between the boxcars.
I can't even remember whether he got off his yell
Before what happened had happened between the boxcars.

But whether or not he managed to get off his yell,
I remember its shape on his mouth, between the boxcars,
And it was shape that yours would be too if you fell
Flat on your ass, on the cinders, between the boxcars.

And there's one sure thing you had better remember well,
You go for the grip at the front, not the back, of the boxcars,
Miss the front, you're knocked off—miss the back, you never
   can tell
But you're flat on your ass, on the cinders, between the
   boxcars.

He was fifteen and old enough to know perfectly well
You go for the grip at the front, not the back, of the boxcars,
But he was the kind of smart aleck you always can tell
Will end flat on his ass, on the cinders, between the boxcars.

Suppose I remembered his name, then what the hell
Good would it do him now between the boxcars?
But it might mean something to me if I could tell
You the name of the one who fell between the boxcars.

Donald Justice

INCIDENT IN A ROSE GARDEN
for Mark Strand

The gardener came running,
An old man, out of breath.
Fear had given him legs.
  Sir, I encountered Death
  Just now among the roses.
  Thin as a scythe he stood there.
  I knew him by his pictures.
  He had his black coat on,
  Black gloves, a broad black hat.
  I think he would have spoken,
  Seeing his mouth stood open.
  Big it was, with white teeth.
  As soon as he beckoned, I ran.
  I ran until I found you.
  Sir, I am quitting my job.
  I want to see my sons
  Once more before I die.
  I want to see California.
We shook hands; he was off.

And there stood Death in the garden,
Dressed like a Spanish waiter.
He had the air of someone
Who because he likes arriving
At all appointments early
Learns to think himself patient.

I watched him pinch one bloom off
And hold it to his nose—
A connoisseur of roses—
One bloom and then another.
They strewed the earth around him.
> Sir, you must be that stranger
> Who threatened my gardener.
> This is my property, sir.
> I welcome only friends here.

Death grinned, and his eyes lit up
With the pale glow of those lanterns
That workmen carry sometimes
To light their way through the dusk.
Now with great care he slid
The glove from his right hand
And held that out in greeting,
A little cage of bone.
> Sir, I knew your father,
> And we were friends at the end.
> As for your gardener,
> I did not threaten him.
> Old men mistake my gestures.
> I only meant to ask him
> To show me to his master.
> I take it you are he?

X. J. Kennedy

LAST LINES ON A WRESTLER

Full-nelsoned in earth's arms the Crusher sleeps
Whom no man living could pin down for keeps.

Guy Owen

EPITAPH FOR A MEAT-PACKER

Here my meat is, clean and dressed,
Newly packaged and expressed;
On the day I'm resurrected,
Angels, stamp me *God-Inspected*.

EPITAPH FOR A BEATNIK POET

Here lies Bogus, beatnik bard,
Who wrote obscenely by the yard;
May he get his just desert
Now that dirt returns to dirt.

Mari Evans

THE REBEL

When I
die
I'm sure
I will have a
Big Funeral . . .
Curiosity
seekers . . .
coming to see
if I
am really
Dead . . .
or just
trying to make
Trouble . . .

Robert Francis

from *EPITAPHS*

Everyman

Preacher or lecher, saint or sot,
What he was once he now is not.

Preacher

He called on God to smite the foe.
Missing his aim, God laid him low.

J. V. Cunningham

EPIGRAM

Friends, on this scaffold Thomas More lies dead
Who would not cut the body from the Head.

Boynton Merrill, Jr.

THE FOSSIL

I am content.
Exhume me
And sleep itself
Will be disturbed.

John Leax

HER SEVENTEENTH WINTER

The old cat whose calm
dwells among us
has taken up residence
by the stove.
Her gums are spotted.
She weighs no more
than her dreams.

She is a seed
of golden fur secured
to the world
by claws honed
on the velvet chair.

Soon a wind will lift
her from the warmth,
and we will find
her gone
into the sleep she dreams.

Sister M. Madeleva, C.S.C.

from *CONCERNING DEATH*

I ASK MY TEACHERS

Why do you wrap your wisdom in a multitude of words?
My master, Death, who will enlighten me completely and
  forever,
Employs no speech at all.

John Stigall

DYING

is like a way
with words,
or a play
on words,
or a flow
of choice words
when

silence is all

that is really
needed.

Off the Page

Richard Wilbur

EPISTEMOLOGY

I

Kick at the rock, Sam Johnson, break your bones:
But cloudy, cloudy is the stuff of stones.

II

We milk the cow of the world, and as we do
We whisper in her ear, "You are not true."

THE PROOF

Shall I love God for causing me to be?
I was mere utterance; shall these words love me?

Yet when I caused his work to jar and stammer,
And one free subject loosened all his grammar,

I love him that he did not in a rage
Once and forever rule me off the page,

But, thinking I might come to please him yet,
Crossed out *delete* and wrote his patient *stet*.

ABOUT THE CONTRIBUTORS

INAMU AMIRI BARAKA [LeRoi Jones] is a poet, novelist, dramatist, short story writer, jazz critic, film maker, and activist. Born LeRoi Jones in Newark, New Jersey in 1934, he graduated from Howard University in 1953, and, after serving in the Air Force, did graduate study at the School of Social Research and Columbia University. He founded the magazine *Yugen*, and helped establish the Black Arts Repertory Theater in Harlem.

COLEMAN BARKS teaches contemporary poetry and creative writing at the University of Georgia. His works include *The Juice* (Harper and Row), *New Words, We're Laughing at the Damage,* and translations of the thirteenth century dervish poet Jalaluddin Rumi. He has won a number of awards including a National Endowment for the Arts Fellowship, The Guy Owen Poetry Prize in 1983, a Pushcart Writer's Choice Award, and the 1986 *New England Review/Bread Loaf Quarterly* Narrative Poem Prize.

DANIEL BERRIGAN was born in 1921 in Virginia, Minnesota. He entered the order of the Jesuits in 1939 and was ordained a Jesuit priest in 1952. His political activities have been vigorous and highly controversial. His many books include *Time Without Number* and *The Geography of Faith*. His awards include the Thomas More Award.

JOHN BERRYMAN, born John Smith in 1914 in McAlester, Oklahoma, was adopted by his mother's second husband and legally named John Berryman. He studied under Mark Van Doren at Columbia University, and received a degree from Clare College, Oxford also. He taught at Wayne State, Harvard, Princeton, and for a number of years at the University of Minnesota. He committed suicide in 1972 by leaping from a bridge in Minneapolis. His honors include the Pulitzer Prize and Bollingen Prize from the Yale University Library, and his books include *The Dispossessed* and *77 Dream Songs*.

EDGAR BOWERS was born in 1924 in Rome, Georgia. He attended Boys' High in Decatur, Georgia and served in the U.S. Army from

1943–1946. He holds a B.A. from the University of North Carolina, Chapel Hill, and a Ph.D. from Stanford University, and has lived in Santa Barbara, California since 1958. His writings include *The Form of Loss*, 1956; *The Astronomers*, 1965; *Living Together*, 1973; and *Witnesses*, 1981. He has received many honors, including membership in the Saucer Club.

KELLY CHERRY was born in Baton Rouge, Louisiana. She is Writer-in-Residence at the University of Wisconsin, Madison. Her writings include novels, *Sick and Full of Burning* (Viking Press), *Augusta Played* (Houghton Mifflin), *In the Wink of an Eye* and *The Lost Traveller's Dream* (Harcourt); and poems, *Relativity* (L.S.U. Press) and *Lovers and Agnostics* (Red Clay). Another book of poems entitled *Natural Theology* is forthcoming from L.S.U. Press. She has won the Canaras Award for fiction from the St. Lawrence University Writers Conference, a National Endowment for the Arts Fellowship, and a Wisconsin Arts Board Fellowship, and has been a Bread Loaf Fellow (1975) and a Yaddo Fellow (1979).

ROBERT CREELEY, born in 1926 in Arlington, Massachusetts, teaches at State University of New York in Buffalo. His writings include *All That Is Lovely in Men, For Love: Poems 1950–1960,* and *Pieces.* He has published fiction as well as poems in periodicals and anthologies. His honors include the Levinson Prize and a Guggenheim Fellowship in poetry.

J(AMES) V(INCENT) CUNNINGHAM was born in 1911 in Cumberland, Maryland, and died in 1985. He taught at Brandeis University. His writings include a major study of Shakespeare, *Woe and Wonder; Tradition and Poetic Structure;* and several volumes of poems. He was awarded a Guggenheim fellowship in poetry, and a National Institute of Arts and Letters grant.

H. D. (HILDA DOOLITTLE) was born in Bethlehem, Pennsylvania in 1886, moving at the age of nine to Philadelphia. A member of the Imagists, a friend of Pound (who suggested or commanded to her the pseudonym H. D.) and Ford Madox Hueffer [Ford], she married Richard Aldington, later was divorced, and spent much of her life in Switzerland. She died in 1961. Her honors include the Brandeis University Creative Arts Award, and an Award of Merit of the American Academy of Arts and Letters. For a while a patient of Freud, she became highly mystical and occult in her later years. Many of her papers are at Yale, and Louis Martz of Yale edited her *Collected Poems*, 1983.

FAZIL HÜSNÜ DAĞLARCA was born in Istanbul in 1914. He was an infantry officer until 1950 and became a labor inspector for the Ministry of Labor in 1952. He founded the literary periodical *Turkce*, and has won numerous prizes. He has published over thirty books of poems, including *The Agony of the West*, 1958; and *Open Sesame, Open*, 1967.

DONALD DAVIE, a British subject born in England in 1922, has since 1968 worked in American universities. Raised a Baptist, he is a member of the Episcopal Church of America. His *Collected Poems, 1950–1970* appeared in 1972, and was followed in 1983 by *Collected Poems, 1970–1983*. He has studied the cultural contribution of the English dissenting churches, especially in the eighteenth century; and he edited *The New Oxford Book of Christian Verse* (1981).

CHRISTOPHER L. DORNIN is a newspaper reporter covering small town politics. He has been an English teacher, an abuse investigator in a school for the retarded, a prison counselor, and a planner for a nursing home chain. He "got the bug" to be a writer in a creative writing course with William Jay Smith at Williams College. "Maybe," he nicely hopes, "I serve God with some of my poems." He lives in Laconia, New Hampshire.

T(HOMAS) S(TEARNS) ELIOT was born in St. Louis, Missouri in 1888. He moved to England in 1945 and was naturalized in 1947. He taught and lectured at many colleges and universities in Europe and the United States. His writings include *Poems by T.S. Eliot* (1919), *Words for Music* (1935), and *The Complete Plays and Poems, 1909–1950* (1952). He received many honors, most notably the Nobel Prize for Literature, the only American poet to receive this award. His posthumous career includes the enormously successful musical *Cats*.

THEODORE ENSLIN's latest book is *The Weather Within* (Inland Press), a poem in a number of parts as homage and, sadly, *monumentum* to George Oppen. He is currently engaged in an investigation of serial possibilities in the composition of poetry. He says that there are relatively few possibilities, but that makes the investigation much more interesting.

MARI EVANS, educator, writer, musician, resides in Indianapolis, Indiana. Formerly Distinguished Writer and Assistant Professor, ASRC, Cornell University, she has taught at Indiana University, Purdue University, Northwestern University, Washington University, St. Louis, and State University of New York at Albany over the past seventeen years. She is the author of numerous articles, four children's books, several performed theatre pieces, two musicals, and three volumes of poetry, including *I Am a Black Woman* and *Nightstar*. She edited the highly acclaimed *Black Woman Writers (1950–1980): A Critical Evaluation*. Her work has been widely anthologized in collections and textbooks.

ROBERT C. FRANCIS, born in Pennsylvania in 1901, has lived in Massachusetts since boyhood and in Amherst since 1926. His first volume of poetry, *Stand With Me Here*, was published in 1936, and since then he has had eighteen other books published. His latest works are *The Trouble with God* (Pennyroyal Press, 1986) and a paperback edition of his *Collected Poems* (University of Massachusetts Press, 1985). He was Phi Beta Kappa poet at Tufts in 1955 and at Harvard in 1960. He lived in Rome 1957–58 and returned to Italy ten years later with an Amy Lowell Poetry Scholarship. Honors include the Rome Prize Fellowship, American Academy of Arts and Letters Shelley Award, and The Academy of American Poets Fellowship for "distinguished poetic achievement" in 1984.

GEORGE GARRETT, born in 1929 in Orlando, Florida, attended Sewanee Military Academy and Princeton (B.A., M.A., Ph.D.). He has taught at Wesleyan University (Connecticut), Rice, the University of South Carolina, and the University of Virginia, where he holds the Henry Hohns Professorship of Creative Writing. He is the author of a play, movies, a number of novels and many short stories and poems. His poems have been collected by the University of Arkansas Press, and his historical novels *The Death of the Fox* and *The Succession* are scholarly and fascinating books.

DIANE GLANCY, born in Kansas City, Missouri, lives in Tulsa, Oklahoma. She is Artist-in-Residence for the State Arts Council of Oklahoma. Several books have been brought out by MyrtleWood Press in Tulsa: *Drystalks of the Moon, Traveling On,* and *West of the Mississippi*. Her most current titles are *Offering* (Holy Cow! Press), *One Age in a*

Dream (Milkweed Chronicle), and *I Tell You Now* (University of Nebraska Press).

O. B. HARDISON, JR. was born in San Diego, California in 1928. He is currently a University Professor of English at Georgetown University, and Director of Washington Resources, Inc. He was Director of the Folger Library for over a decade. He has published a number of books, including *The Enduring Monument: Praise in Renaissance Literary Theory and Practice, Christian Rite and Christian Drama in the Middle Ages*, and *Pro Musica Antiqua* (poems). He is an editor of the *Princeton Encyclopedia of Poetry and Poetics*, currently being revised. His many honors include the Haskins Medal of the Medieval Academy, the Cavaliere Ufficiale (Italian decoration), and the Order of the British Empire.

ROGER HECHT, born in New York City in 1926, still lives there. His writings include *27 Poems* (1966); *Signposts* (1970); *Parade of Ghosts* (1976) and *Burnt Offerings* (1979), both published by The Lightning Tree, Santa Fe, New Mexico; and *A Quarrelling of Dust* (1986). His work is represented in several anthologies and journals. He is a member of the Poetry Society of America. His "War Memento," like other literary masterpieces, reads beautifully aloud.

M. L. HESTER was born in 1947, and educated at Guilford College and the University of North Carolina at Greensboro. He is a free-lance writer and editor of Tudor Publishers, Inc., a small press in Greensboro. He has published novels under pen names.

LEROI JONES now prefers the name Inamu Amiri Baraka; see his biography under that entry.

DONALD JUSTICE was born in 1925 in Miami, Florida. He teaches at the University of Florida. He is married to the writer Jean Ross Justice. They have one son. His works include *The Summer Anniversaries, Night Light, Departures, Selected Poems*, and *The Sunset Maker*, as well as a collection of literary criticism, *Platonic Scripts*. He has many honors, including a Guggenheim Fellowship, the Pulitzer Prize in Poetry, and membership in the Saucer Club.

X. J. KENNEDY was born in Dover, New Jersey, in 1929. Until 1979 he was a Professor of English at Tufts. He is now a free-lance writer when not visiting colleges as a lecturer or reader of poetry. His works include the college textbook *An Introduction to Poetry* (1966; sixth ed., 1986), some children's books *(Brats,* 1986, and others), and his latest collection of poetry, *Cross Ties: Selected Poems* (1985). He has contributed poems to many journals and reviews. Honors include the Lamont Award of the Academy of American Poets, the 1985 Los Angeles Times book award for poetry, the Shelley Memorial Award. He has also been a Phi Beta Kappa poet.

JOHN LEAX, Poet-in-Residence at Houghton College, where he has taught since 1968, has published poems in *Southern Poetry Journal, Tennessee Poetry Journal, Greenfield Review, Karamu, Nimrod, Midwest Quarterly,* and many other journals. His publications include *Reaching into Silence* (Shaw, 1974) and *The Task of Adam* (Zondervan, 1985). He writes that he is a "gardener, woodcutter, fisherman, nuclear pacifist, and would-be ecologist" and that his work, including his prose journal *In Season and Out,* frequently reflects such concerns.

PETER LEVI was born in 1931 in Ruislip, Middlesex, England. In 1984 he was elected Professor of Poetry at Oxford University. Until 1977 he was a Jesuit priest; he is now married and lives near Oxford, where he is a fellow of St. Catherine's College. He is a classicist whose writing includes three uncategorizable books on modern Greece, Afghanistan, and the English landscape—as well as translations, critical and scholarly works, and a thriller.

JANET LEWIS has as her most recent publication *The Swans,* a libretto, published by John Daniel, Santa Barbara, 1986. Swallow/Ohio University Press has re-issued a novel, *Against a Darkening Sky,* originally published in 1943, and a short-story collection, *Goodbye, Son and Other Stories,* originally published in 1946. An opera-oratorio entitled *The Legend* has been made from her novel *The Invasion.* She is the widow of Yvor Winters, q.v. Her historical novels, including *The Wife of Martin Guerre* and *The Trial of Soren Quist,* are models of style, lucidity, thoughtful scholarship, and grace. So are her poems.

JOHN LOGAN was born in 1923 in Red Oak, Iowa. He studied at Coe College, the State University of Iowa, Georgetown University, and Notre Dame. He has taught at St. John's College, Notre Dame, the University of Washington, San Francisco State, and the State University of

New York, Buffalo. His books include *A Cycle for Mother Cabrini* (Grove), *The Anonymous Lover* (Liveright), and *The House that Jack Built*. He has been a Guggenheim fellow and poetry editor for *Nation* and *Critic*.

ARCHIBALD MACLEISH was born in 1892 in Glencoe, Illinois. He lived for many years in Conway, Massachusetts. Besides teaching at various universities, he served as Assistant Secretary of State in 1944–45. He received the Pulitzer Prize for poetry twice. Other honors include the Shelley Memorial Award for poetry and the Bollingen Prize from the Yale University Library. His works include among others *Poems, 1924–1933, Conquistador, Frescoes for Mr. Rockefeller's City*, the play *J.B.*, and *Collected Poems 1917–1952*. He died in 1982.

JOHN MACOUBRIE (1925–1983) was a native of Oregon and a graduate of Reed College. He had a degree in social work and spent most of his adult life in Minneapolis. Some of his friends are planning to publish a small volume of his poems.

SISTER M. MADELEVA was born Mary Evaline Wolff in Cumberland, Wisconsin in 1887. She studied at several American colleges and universities and at Oxford University. She was a member of The Congregation of the Holy Cross, and President of St. Mary's College, Notre Dame, Indiana, from 1945 to 1961. She died in 1964. Her works include *Collected Poems, The Four Last Things*, and *My First Seventy Years* (an autobiography), all published by Macmillan, which is issuing another volume of her poems in 1987. Her many honors include the Siena Medal, the Woman of Achievement Award, the Campion Award, and honorary degrees from Mount Mary College, Manhattan College, the University of Notre Dame, Manhattanville College of the Sacred Heart, and Indiana University.

ROLAND MATHIAS was born in 1915 in Talybont-on-Usk, Wales. He is a former Grammar School Headmaster, and since 1969 has been a free-lance writer and lecturer. His writings include *Days Enduring and Other Poems* (1943), *Break in Harvest* (1946), *The Roses of Tretower* (1952), *The Flooded Valley* (1960), *Absalom in the Tree* (1971), *Snipe's Castle* (1979), and *Burning Brambles: Selected Poems* (1983). His *Anglo-Welsh Literature: An Illustrated History* is scheduled for 1987. He won prizes for poetry in 1972 and 1980.

214

SISTER MAURA is a School Sister of Notre Dame, and Professor of English at the College of Notre Dame. She has published poetry and prose in various journals, and several books of poetry, *What We Women Know* (Sparrow Press) being the most recent.

VICTORIA MCCABE, born in Clare, Iowa, in 1948, currently teaches writing at Regis College in Denver. Her writings include *John Keats Porridge: Favorite Recipes of Contemporary American Poets*. She is widely published in *Poetry Now, American Poetry Review, University of Windsor Review, Prairie Schooner, Hollins Critic*, and elsewhere. Awards and honors she has won, among others, are the Stephens Colorado Poetry Contest and the Hallmark Honor Prize. Her husband works with addicts in a recovery program. Her sons' names are Shannon Ezra and Keegan Michael.

PHYLLIS MCGINLEY was born in 1905 in Ontario, Oregon. She was a member of the National Institute of Arts and Letters and the Poetry Society of America. Her works include *Husbands Are Difficult: or, The Book of Oliver Ames* (1941), *Times Three: Selected Verse From Three Decades* (1960), and several juvenile books. She received the Edna St. Vincent Millay Memorial Award of the Poetry Society of America (1955), the Golden Book Award, and the Pulitzer Prize for poetry, as well as other awards. She died in 1978.

BOYNTON MERRILL, JR. was born in 1925 in Boston, Massachusetts. He was educated at Deerfield Academy and Dartmouth College, from which he received a B.A. in English. He lives in Henderson, Kentucky, where he is a farmer and realtor. He is the author of *Jefferson's Nephews: A Frontier Tragedy* (Princeton University Press and, second edition, University Press of Kentucky).

THOMAS MERTON was born in 1915 in Prades, France. He entered the Abbey of Gethsemane, Kentucky, and became a Trappist monk in 1941, took solemn vows in 1947, and was ordained a priest in 1949. He taught at the Abbey from 1951–65. He died in 1968. His writings include *The Seven Storey Mountain, Thirty Poems, Selected Poems*, and *Raids on the Unspeakable*, among others. He was awarded the Columbia University Medal for Excellence and an honorary degree from the University of Kentucky.

VASSAR MILLER was born in 1924 in Houston, Texas, where she has lived all her life. She began her writing as a child, fascinated by rhymes and wordplay. She did a thesis on the mysticism in the poetry of Edwin Arlington Robinson at the University of Houston. She has taught creative writing at St. John's School and has been writer-in-residence at the University of St. Thomas. Her poetry was nominated for the Pulitzer Prize in 1961 and 1985, and three of her books have won the annual poetry prize of the Texas Institute of Letters. *Library Journal* called her *Selected and New Poems 1950–1980* "the best small press book of poetry for 1982." Her poems have been translated into Spanish and published in Latin American journals. Recently she edited an anthology of poetry and fiction by and about those handicapped with motor and sensory dysfunctions.

N(AVARRE) SCOTT MOMADAY was born in 1934 in Lawton, Oklahoma, son of Kiowa artist Alfred Morris Momaday and writer Natchee Scott, and grew up on Indian reservations of the American Southwest, including the Navajo, the Apache (Jicarilla and San Carlos), and the Pueblo (Jemez). He is currently a Professor of English at the University of Arizona. His writings include *House Made of Dawn* (1968), *Colorado: Summer, Fall, Winter, Spring* (1976), and *The Names* (1976). His awards include a Guggenheim Fellowship, the Pulitzer Prize, The National Institute of Arts and Letters Award, and numerous honorary degrees.

HARRY MORRIS continues to live a bucolic existence, tempering the rigors of academic and literary pursuits with his hobbies: herpet-, ornith-, and entomology. So he informs the editor, who adds that Harry Morris' book *Last Things in Shakespeare* (Florida State University Press, 1985) is one of the most important books of Shakespearean scholarship and criticism in this century.

EDWIN MUIR was born in 1877 in Orkney, and died in Cambridge, England in 1959. He was a contributor to the *New English Weekly*, and a Norton Lecturer at Harvard. His *Collected Poems* in two editions were published by Oxford University Press. T. S. Eliot wrote, justly, of him, "Edwin Muir will remain among the poets who have added glory to the English language."

HOWARD NEMEROV's recent publications include *Inside the Onion* (poems), University of Chicago Press, 1984, and *New and Selected Es-*

216

says, Southern Illinois Press, 1985. Forthcoming is *The Oak in the Acorn*, a study of Proust, Louisiana State University Press. He is the first recipient of the Aiken Taylor Award.

FRANK O'HARA was born in 1926 in Baltimore, Maryland. He worked at the Museum of Modern Art from 1955 until his death in 1966. His works include *The Collected Poems of Frank O'Hara, A City Winter,* and *Other Poems.* He won the Hopwood Award for Poetry in 1951, and was a co-winner of the National Book Award in 1972.

ELDER OLSON was born in 1909. He is Distinguished Service Professor Emeritus of English Language and Literature, The University of Chicago. He is the author of numerous books of poetry, criticism, etc., the latest of which is *Last Poems.*

GUY OWEN, poet, novelist, and critic, grew up on a farm in the Cape Fear region of North Carolina. He received three degrees, including a Ph.D. from the University of North Carolina at Chapel Hill. His teaching career included assignments at Davidson College, Elon College, Stetson University, and North Carolina State University. He founded and was the original editor of *Southern Poetry Review.* At State, he was perhaps best known for his courses in creative writing and best beloved for the generosity with which he helped aspiring writers, both students and others. Guy Owen died on July 23, 1981. He was fifty-six years old.

LINDA PASTAN was born in 1932 in New York City. She is a poet noted for wit and precision, severity and tenderness. W. W. Norton is her primary publisher. Her books of poetry include *A Perfect Circle of Sun, Aspects of Eve, Waiting for My Life, The Five Stages of Grief, PM/ AM,* and *A Fraction of Darkness.*

PAUL RAMSEY was born in Atlanta, Georgia in 1924, served as a naval officer in World War II, received his Ph.D. from the University of Minnesota, and is an Associate Editor of *The Upstart Crow* and President of the DuLeslin Agency (literary agency). He has published several scholarly and critical books and short fiction as well as books of poems, and has taught at several schools. In 1981 he was Research Fellow at Yale University. As editor of the anthology, he has in this note chosen to stick to clearly verifiable truths, including the truth that he has very much enjoyed the considerable labor of making this anthology.

217

BELLE RANDALL was born in 1940 in Ellensburg , Washington, and lives in Seattle, Washington. She studied at the University of California (Berkeley) and Stanford University, where she held a Wallace Stagner Fellowship. She teaches at Cornish Institute in Seattle and does a Prosody Workshop at the Centrum Writers Conference. Her works include *101 Different Ways of Playing Solitaire* (University of Pittsburgh Press) and *Orpheus Sedan* (Copper Canyon Press).

JULIA RANDALL was born in 1923. She received degrees from Bennington College and Johns Hopkins University. She has retired from teaching at Hollins College, Virginia to her native Baltimore County, Maryland. Her awards include two from the National Endowment for the Arts and the Shelley Award. Her sixth book of poems, *Moving in Memory*, has been published by Louisiana State University Press (1987), and she has completed a book of poems for children entitled *Sometimes Up and Sometimes Down*.

JOHN RAVEN is a native of Washington, D.C. He lived in New York, briefly, during his early years, and was captured by the excitement and diversity of that city. He returned in 1960, and has lived there since. He served in the United States Air Force for four years. Writing, he says, has been a part of his life for as long as he can remember.

DAVID RAY has many publications, including *The Touched Life: New and Selected Poems* (Scarecrow Press), and poems for his late son entitled *Sam's Book* (Wesleyan University Press, 1987). He teaches at the University of Missouri-Kansas City. In 1986, for the fifth successive year, he won a PEN Syndicated Fiction Award. In 1987 he is a visiting professor at the University of Otago in Dunedin, New Zealand.

I(VOR) A(RMSTRONG) RICHARDS was born in 1893 in Sandbach, England, and lived for several years in Cambridge, England. He taught at Harvard and died in 1979. His writings include *The Meaning of Meaning, Goodbye Earth and Other Poems, Internal Colloquies: Poems and Plays, The Screens and Other Poems,* and *New and Selected Poems.* His many honors include the King's Medal for poetry, and the Russell Loines Award for poetry from the National Institute of Arts and Letters.

EDOUARD RODITI has published poetry since the early 1930's, including a collection published by New Directions in 1949. *Thrice Cho-*

sen (Black Sparrow Press, 1981) is a collection of verse gathered from five decades of Roditi's thought. In this collection we learn of Roditi's peculiar geography: born in Paris of American parents, educated internationally, resident for the most part in Paris but often located elsewhere, and during the Second World War apparently a yearning exile in Kansas City.

THEODORE ROETHKE was born in 1908 in Saginaw, Michigan. He was a Professor of English and Poet-in-Residence at the University of Washington, Seattle, until his death in 1963. He was a member of the National Institute of Arts and Letters, Phi Beta Kappa, Phi Kappa Phi, and Chi Phi. His works include *Words for the Wind, Sequence, Sometimes Metaphysical, Straw for the Fire,* and *The Far Field.* Among his many awards are a Guggenheim Fellowship, the National Institute of Arts and Letters Award, and the Pulitzer Prize for poetry.

DAVID ROSENBERG has a growing reputation as a result of several volumes of poetry and translation, including the very well-received Poet's Bible Series. His periodical publications include *Harper's Magazine, New Republic,* and *Paris Review.* His book *Chosen Days: Celebrating Jewish Festivals in Poetry and Art,* with decorations by Leonard Baskin, was published by Doubleday. He lives in New York City.

ERNEST SANDEEN is Emeritus Professor of English at the University of Notre Dame. His poems have appeared in *Poetry, New Yorker, Iowa Review, Prism International, Saturday Review,* and other publications. His books include, among other works, *Children and Older Strangers, Like Any Road Anywhere,* and *Collected Poems, 1953–1977.*

KARL SHAPIRO was born in 1913 in Baltimore, Maryland. He is a Professor of English at the University of California. He is a member of the National Institute of Arts and Letters and Phi Beta Kappa. His writings include *Collected Poems, 1948–1978, White-Haired Lover,* and others. His many awards include the Pulitzer Prize for poetry, the Shelley Memorial Prize, and the Bollingen Prize from the Yale University Library.

ROBERT B. SHAW studied at Harvard and Yale (Ph.D.) and teaches at Mount Holyoke College. His publications include poems, for instance *Comforting the Wilderness* (Wesleyan University Press), a study of Herbert and Donne entitled *The Call of God* (Cowley Publications), an edition of Henry Vaughan, a libretto for a performed opera, and numerous essays.

MYRA SKLAREW has been writing poetry and prose with a primary focus on poetry since 1942. She has a background in scientific research, music, and art. Her writings include *The Travels of the Itinerant Freda Aharon* (Water Mark Press), *The Science of Goodbyes* (University of Georgia Press), and *Altamira* (poems—WWPH, 1987); *At the Door to That Room* (short fiction—Lost Roads Press 1987). She is Director of Yaddo. Her awards include the Di Castagnola Award and a National Endowment for the Arts Fellowship. She wrote in response to our request for information, "If you wish something about the life of the spirit, I could supply that. . . . I am learning not to be present, though I always bring my body, which is punctual, attentive, and responsible."

FRANCIS J. SMITH, born in 1920 in Lorain, Ohio, is a Jesuit priest. He was educated at Oxford and is a Professor of English at John Carroll University in Cleveland, Ohio. He has published in many national magazines such as *Chicago Tribune Magazine, Manhattan Poetry Review, America,* and *Long Pond Review.* He has published two volumes of poetry, *First Prelude* (Loyola University Press) and *All Is a Prize* (Pterodactyl Press). He is a member of the Poetry Society of America and of Poets and Writers, Inc.

PAUL SMYTH was born in 1944 in Boston, Massachusetts. He received his B.A. from Harvard in 1968. He is a free-lance poet and fiction writer. His writings include *The Cardinal Sins: A Beastiary* (1981), *Antibodies* (1979), and *Thistles and Thorns* (1977). He has recently finished a novel and has not yet finished the renovation of an eighteenth century house in Cummington, Massachusetts.

ANN STANFORD is a Professor of English at California State University, Northridge. She is the author of seven books of poetry, translator of the *Bhagavad Gita,* contributor to numerous anthologies, and critic.

TIMOTHY STEELE has two collections of poems, *Uncertainties and Rest* (Louisiana State University Press, 1979) and *Sapphics against Anger* (Random House, 1986). *Missing Measures,* a historical study of the ideas and conditions that contributed to modern experimental verse, is forthcoming from Stanford University Press.

JOHN STIGALL was born in Chattanooga, Tennessee. He left home at the age of seventeen and moved to Harlem. He graduated from the State University of New York. He is Assistant Professor of English at Chattanooga State Technical Community College. He is married to the former Miss Iris Starks; they have one child, John, Jr. His poem "Dying" is from *In Avant-Gardens* (Damballah Press).

FRANCIS SULLIVAN is a Jesuit priest. He has published two volumes of poetry, *Table Talk with the Recent God* (Paulist Press, 1974) and *Spy Wednesday's Kind* (The Smith, 1979), and one volume of translations, *Lyric Psalms: Half A Psalter* (Pastoral Press, 1983). He is currently writing Anglo-Saxon type riddles for stage presentation to music and dance, and also translating the tracts of Bartolome de las Casas (1484–1566) who was the defender of the American natives against the Spanish Conquest. He teaches at Boston College and the Gregorian University, Rome.

ALLEN TATE was born in 1899 in Winchester, Kentucky, and died in Nashville, Tennessee in 1979. An Agrarian and New Critic, friend of Ransom and Eliot and many another prominent writer, he was very much the man of letters in the modern world, biographer, social and literary critic, poet, novelist, and mentor and friend to many. He was a Regent's Professor of English at the University of Minnesota. His writings include biographies of Stonewall Jackson and Jefferson Davis, *Reactionary Essays, Reason in Madness, The Forlorn Demon, On the Limits of Poetry, Collected Poems*, and others. Among his awards and honors are a Guggenheim Fellowship, the Brandeis University Medal Award for Poetry, and the Bollingen Prize from the Yale University Library.

R(ONALD) S(TEWART) THOMAS was born in 1913 in Cardiff, Wales. He was ordained a deacon of the Anglican Church in 1936, ordained a priest in 1937, and has served as a vicar of St. Hywyn, Aberdaron with St. Mary, Bodferin. His works include *Laboratories of the Spirit, Words and the Poet*, and *Selected Poems 1964–1968*. He received the Heinemann Award in 1955, the Queens Gold Medal for Poetry in 1964, and the Welsh Arts Council Award in 1968.

ROBERT WALLACE teaches at Case Western Reserve University. His most recent collection of poems is *Girlfriends and Wives* (Carnegie-Mellon University Press, 1984). A volume of his selected and new poems entitled *The Lost History of Everything* is scheduled for the fall of 1987. He has also written an excellent textbook, *Writing Poems*, and is editor of *Light Year*, the annual which helps to brighten the literary glooms of our time.

ROBERT PENN WARREN was born in 1905 in south Kentucky, in a town called Guthrie. Since his college days at Vanderbilt University, he has divided his time between academic interests and writing, chiefly poetry. Since the 1940's, he has devoted himself, except for a period of teaching at Yale for one term a year, to writing. He has published some eight or nine novels, fifteen volumes of poetry, and some criticism. He is the first Poet Laureate of the United States.

RICHARD WILBUR was born in 1921 in New York City. He is writer-in-residence at Smith College, Northampton, Massachusetts. Among his many awards and honors are the Edna St. Vincent Millay Memorial Award (1957), Pulitzer Prize for poetry and National Book Award for poetry (both 1957), and the Shelley Memorial Award (1973). His writings include *The Mind Reader: New Poems* (1976), *Responses: Prose Pieces, 1953–1976*, and *Seed Leaves: Homage to R. F.* (1974).

WILLIAM CARLOS WILLIAMS was born in 1883 in Rutherford, New Jersey. He was a poet, playwright, novelist, essayist, and physician. He had a private medical practice in Rutherford until 1951. His works include *Selected Poems* (1976), *Pictures from Brueghel and Other Poems* (1962), and *I Wanted to Write a Poem: The Autobiography of the Works of a Poet* (1958). In 1926 he was awarded the Dial Award for distinguished service to American Literature. Other honors include National Book Award for poetry, the Bollingen Prize from the Yale University Library, and the Pulitzer Prize in poetry.

YVOR WINTERS was a poet of high achievement and a vigorous and important defender of the moral importance and nature of literature. A beautiful metrist himself, he taught persuasively that meter is morality; and the editor of this anthology is grateful for his labors. The last work published during his lifetime was *Forms of Discovery*, 1967. Since his death *The Collected Poems of Yvor Winters* was brought out by Carcanet, Manchester in 1978 and by Swallow/Ohio University Press in America. Published in 1973 was *The Uncollected Essays and Reviews of Yvor Winters*, edited by Francis Murphy.

222

KAROL WOJTYLA (Pope John Paul II) was born in 1920 in Wadowice, Poland. He served as archbishop of Krakow and as a Roman Catholic cardinal before his election as Pope in 1978. He has been a professor of moral theology at the University of Krakow and the University of Lublin. Writing under the pseudonym Andrzej Jawien, he published several volumes of poetry and a play. Other writings include *Fruitful and Responsible Love* (1979), *Easter Vigil and Other Poems* (1979), and *You Are My Favorites* (1980).

INDEX OF AUTHORS AND TITLES

226